P9-CQL-838

PSYCHO

ALSO BY JANET LEIGH:

THERE REALLY WAS A HOLLYWOOD

ALSO BY CHRISTOPHER NICKENS:

ELIZABETH TAYLOR
BETTE DAVIS
NATALIE WOOD
MARLON BRANDO

BY CHRISTOPHER NICKENS AND JAMES SPADA

STREISAND: THE WOMAN AND THE LEGEND

PSYCHO

BEHIND THE SCENES
OF THE CLASSIC THRILLER

JANET LEIGH

WITH CHRISTOPHER NICKENS

Harmony Books / New York

Published by Harmony Books, a division of Crown Publishers, Inc., 201 East 50th Street, New York, New York 10022. Member of the Crown Publishing Group.

Random House, Inc., New York, Toronto, London, Sydney, Auckland

HARMONY and colophon are trademarks of Crown Publishers, Inc.

Manufactured in the United States of America

Library of Congress Cataloging-in-Publication Data

Leigh, Janet.
Psycho: behind the scenes of the classic thriller / by Janet Leigh with Christopher Nickens.—1st ed.
p.   cm.
Includes bibliographical references.
1. Psycho (Motion picture) I. Nickens, Christopher. II. Title.
PN1997.P793L45   1995
791.43'72—dc20
94-47269
CIP

ISBN 0-517-70112-X

10 9 8 7 6 5 4 3 2 1

First Edition

For Alfred Hitchcock
and Anthony Perkins

CONTENTS

AN OPENING NOTE

Are you wondering why I waited thirty-five years to do a book on *Psycho*? I don't blame you. I've been asking myself the same question. The odd thing is that it wasn't even my idea that started the ball rolling. Well, wait a minute. Let's back up and I'll try to explain how this all came about.

First, a project like this would never have occurred to me when we were making *Psycho* because no one, especially me, knew that this movie would assume the mantle of a classic and take its place in film history.

Some years went by after *Psycho*'s release, but it maintained a high level of intense interest among moviegoers. So authors, chroniclers, and analysts began to include the movie in their books on the cinema's most memorable films. And, of course, *Psycho* was discussed in the numerous volumes dedicated to the exploration of the life and works of Alfred Hitchcock. But I saw no reason for Janet Leigh to jump into those crowded waters.

More time elapsed, and still the scrutiny and excitement surrounding *Psycho* persisted. I was interviewed a great deal regarding the film, and more literature on it was published. I was spending less and less time in front of the camera—but amazingly enough, the fan mail continued to pour in. Moviegoers listed many of the pictures I had been in as among their personal favorites, but *Psycho* was almost always at the top of their lists. It was—and still is—fulfilling to have this labor of love so recognized and appreciated—particularly after we lost Mr. Hitchcock, and then later, Anthony Perkins.

As I limited my time in front of the camera, I increased my time behind a desk—writing. I wrote my autobiography, *There Really Was a Hollywood,* and found that my thoughts flowed easily onto paper. I had an idea for a novel, so I really bit the bullet and devoted a few years to nurturing the concept into reality, *House of Destiny.*

During this period, I was constantly asked to do personal appearances. One of them was in Orlando, Florida, at the Universal Theme Park, which, among a myriad of other attractions, houses a Hitchcock Pavilion. There was a convention of thousands. And I sat for hours signing photos as the people filed out of the Hitchcock exhibit.

From Florida I went to New York on business, and during a luncheon with some friends from the literary world, I mentioned my visit to Orlando. We marveled at the longevity of *Psycho*'s appeal. And a brainstorm struck them: They thought I should do a book about the phenomenon of *Psycho*.

I dismissed the idea—what more could be written about *Psycho*? About Hitchcock? About Perkins? But then we began to discuss the effect of this film later—*thirty-three years later!* The effect on the participants, their families, and the public. And I was hooked.

As I started to do research, I realized there was indeed a great deal more to say about *Psycho*. Over the months, each interview with a colleague, each bit of information gathered from countless sources made me realize how complex, rich, and resourceful this classic is. Until the very last page of this book, I was still discovering new insights into the people involved in all aspects of the picture, into the film itself, and into the general public's depth of feeling about it.

I don't believe I would have been able to write this earlier. I hope I've grown into it at last.

Janet Leigh

PROLOGUE

Although the offer to work with Janet on this book came out of the proverbial blue, I accepted it immediately and with great enthusiasm. As a lifelong movie buff I was, naturally, a devotee of Alfred Hitchcock's remarkable films—particularly *Psycho*. And ever since seeing *Houdini* as a youngster, I have been an admirer of Janet's as well, not only because of her warm, attractive screen personality but because she seemed to tackle, with apparent ease, so many diverse and interesting roles.

At a time when many actresses were content to rely solely on looks and sex appeal in order to forge and maintain a movie career, Janet, who could easily have done the same, desired—and managed to *deliver*—much more. Because of this willingness to test her talents, her acting resume includes a unique mix of movies. In her filmography, popular "popcorn" crowd pleasers rub shoulders with critically acclaimed classics.

A few years ago, the *Los Angeles Times* published a list of what it considered to be the fifty greatest movies of all time. Janet found she was the only actress to have appeared in three of them: *Psycho,* John Frankenheimer's *The Manchurian Candidate,* and Orson Welles's *Touch of Evil.*

In addition to the inherent fun of working on a project about a truly great film with one of my favorite actresses, I felt this book would offer Janet and me an opportunity to reflect on the influence and impact *Psycho* continues to have, while at the same time allowing us to set the record straight, as it were, by correcting some of the myths, misconceptions, and outright lies that have clung to the picture—like a wet shower curtain—for thirty-five years.

The Italian advertising art.

In a recent poll of film critics and movie fans in France, the shower murder in *Psycho* was voted the single most famous scene in motion picture history. While such results are, of course, always arguable, few film historians in the world could suggest a much worthier choice.

Indeed, the completely unexpected, horrifying stabbing death of Marion Crane in the bathroom of cabin one at the Bates Motel has become a genuine icon of the cinema, a scene of such enduring impact that it has taken on a pop-culture life of its own: Every camera angle, every close-up, every edit, every note of the screeching violin score that accompanies the murder has been blatantly stolen (or copied in homage, depending on your viewpoint) and satirized in countless subsequent movies, stage parodies, situation comedies, and even television commercials. (Since 1960, has any director filmed water shooting out of a showerhead from any viewpoint except in the dead-on manner that Hitchcock devised?)

But one brief scene, no matter how stunning, does not guarantee a classic. The indelible image, for example, of Marilyn Monroe standing astride a subway vent with her white skirt billowing provocatively around her thighs is one of the most recognizable movie moments of all time, a symbol of Hollywood in every corner of the world. But its fame is due more to still photographs taken of the occasion than to the scene itself, and the film that contains it, *The Seven Year Itch,* is a talky, bland sex comedy that would surely have faded from memory had it not starred Monroe.

Psycho, however, has a lot more to recommend it than just the shower scene. Like a handful of other films (most notably *Citizen Kane*) that are able to captivate audiences and influence filmmakers decade after decade, *Psycho* is a masterful blend of various cinematic elements that add up to a mesmerizing, timeless whole. Critic Richard Schickel calls the film "one of the crucial cultural artifacts of this era."

The unique plotline, its unexpected twists (including a hair-raising second murder sequence), the atmospheric art direction and brilliant, innovative cinematography, the surging, unsettling musical score, Hitchcock's artful direction, and the vivid performances of Janet Leigh and Anthony Perkins all contribute to the picture's lasting, universal appeal.

In many ways the genesis and subsequent box-office success of *Psycho* can be attributed to the electronic monster that struck terror in the hearts of every studio head in the 1950s: television.

Alfred Hitchcock's early success in his native England with such popular and critically acclaimed pictures as *The Lodger, The 39 Steps,* and *The Lady Vanishes* inevitably brought him to the attention of Hollywood, where he re-located in 1939, under contract to producer David O. Selznick, who was preparing the release of *Gone With the Wind.* Hitchcock's first American film, *Rebecca,* was voted an Academy Award as 1940's Best Picture, and it quickly established the director as "the Master of Suspense."

Subsequent Hitchcock hits included *Suspicion, Saboteur, Shadow of a Doubt, Lifeboat, Spellbound,* and *Notorious.* After a brief dry spell in the late forties, Hitch sailed into the next decade at the top of his form with *Strangers on a Train,* and went on to create such memorable films as *Dial M for Murder, Rear Window, To Catch a Thief, The Man Who Knew Too Much* (a remake of his 1934 British production), *Vertigo,* and *North by Northwest.*

But for all of the renown his thirty-year career as a filmmaker brought him, it couldn't compare to the fame he experienced when he decided to, as he put it, "dabble" in television in 1955.

On October 2, *Alfred Hitchcock Presents* debuted over the CBS network and immediately shot to the top of the ratings lists, where it remained for most of its ten-year run. With a formal, British-accented "Good evening," Hitchcock introduced each weekly installment of the mystery anthology (he also directed several episodes), and his droll put-downs of the show's sponsors delighted millions of viewers. His signature entrance—in rotund profile and shadow against a musical backdrop of Gounod's *Funeral March of a Marionette*—has remained one of the most identifiable images in the medium's history.

"It was unbelievable how famous that show made him," recalls his daughter, Patricia Hitchcock O'Connell. "I think it had been on for a little over a year when we went to Tahiti for a vacation. We were on this quiet, secluded little beach, and all of a sudden people swarmed out of nowhere to see him. It was like being with Elvis Presley!" (Hitchcock would take tremendous advantage of this TV-fed fame when it came time to promote *Psycho*.)

In addition to high-profile celebrity status, *Alfred Hitchcock Presents* also brought its namesake untold millions with which to indulge his well-known taste for fine art and rare wines. As the 1950s drew to a close, Hitchcock was numbered among the wealthiest director/producers in Hollywood. Ironically, it was at this time that he decided to forsake the lush budgets, glossy production values, and costly superstars that he had relied on for the bulk of his recent films.

Always eager to keep on top of trends in the movie industry, Hitchcock noted with keen interest how many cheaply made black-and-white thrillers (with particular appeal to the highly lucrative teenage market that had burgeoned in the postwar years) were cleaning up at the box office. Such budget-conscious independent filmmakers as William Castle and Roger Corman had tapped into this growing audience with exploitation films in the horror and science fiction genres. A maverick showman as well as a director, Castle was notorious for the gimmicks he implemented to attract impressionable young audiences: He flew skeletons over moviegoers' heads, installed phony nurses in theater lobbies to tend to horror-stricken patrons, and wired seats to set off mild electrical shocks to better enhance the (few) scary moments in his pictures.

Drive-in marquees of the fifties trumpeted such fare as *Attack of the 50 Ft. Woman, The Incredible Shrinking Man, The Blob, Earth vs. the Flying Saucers, The Fly,* and other science fiction titles as well as shockers anchored firmly on earth: *The Brain That Wouldn't Die, House on Haunted Hill, Dementia, The Tingler, The Unearthly,* and *Macabre.* Many of these efforts—along with the infamous films of Ed Wood—have become camp classics, but at the time, they were roundly dismissed by critics, who labeled many of them "bargain-basement Hitchcock." The profits they accrued, however, couldn't be denied, and following the expensive production of *North by Northwest,* Hitchcock began looking around early in 1959 for a property that would allow him the opportunity to beat his cheapjack imitators at their own game.

As with many of our greatest films, *Psycho* began life as a novel, and it's been reported as fact that the book by Robert Bloch, which evolved into one of the most terrifying films of all time, was brought to Hitchcock's attention by his mild-mannered production assistant of twenty years, Peggy Robertson.

"I wish I *could* lay claim to finding *Psycho,*" Robertson laughs today. "But the truth is every Monday morning Hitch and I used to read the *New York Times Book Review.* Hitch really liked the reviews of Anthony Boucher, who covered the new arrivals in crime fiction. And this one Monday, Hitch said, 'Boucher is raving about this book, *Psycho.*' He wanted to know if Paramount (with whom Hitchcock had a production deal) had seen the book and/or covered it. 'Covered' meant that the story department had read the novel and prepared a synopsis."

Script reader William Pinkard *had* covered *Psycho* for Paramount following submission of the novel by Robert Bloch's agent in February 1959, and while he admired its originality, he warned that it would be "impossible for films."(Robertson doesn't recall if she or her boss ever saw Pinkard's synopsis and appraisal.)

Hitch and Robertson were so distracted by the editing chores on *North by Northwest* at MGM that they forgot about *Psycho* for a while. "Then, when Hitch was at the airport on the way to London to scout locations for *No Bail for the Judge*, a film we were planning for Audrey Hepburn that fell through, he called me and said, 'Get a hold of *Psycho*.' By that time he had read it. 'It's excellent,' he added. 'I think we better get it right away.' So from that point on, it was in the hands of the agents."

Existing paperwork shows that Alfred Hitchcock paid a measly $9,000 to acquire the movie rights to *Psycho*. It was a shockingly low figure—even by 1959 standards—for a title that would go on to become the most lucrative in the entire Hitchcock canon.

"It could have been worse," Robert Bloch said in his final interview prior to his death in September 1994. "The original offer was for five thousand dollars."

When agent Ned Brown, acting on Hitchcock's behalf, contacted Bloch's agent, Harry Altshuler, it was with a casual bid from a client who wished to remain anonymous. Bloch had never sold one of his stories to the movies, and he trusted Altshuler to negotiate the best deal. "We got them up to seventy-five hundred," Bloch said, "but we still didn't know who the potential buyer was." Bloch wanted to press for $10,000, but Altshuler advised him ultimately to settle for the $9,000 offer. After Bloch's publisher, Simon & Schuster, took 15 percent off the top of the deal and Altshuler collected his 10 percent commission, Bloch—who was "flabbergasted" when he learned it was Hitchcock who had been doing the bidding—cleared "about six thousand seven hundred fifty dollars before taxes."

In fact, although *Psycho* is Robert Bloch's greatest claim to immortality, it never proved to be much of a financial windfall for him. He had only received an advance of $750 for the novel to begin with, and despite the enormous box-office receipts generated by the movie, Bloch never received any "thank you" bonuses from Hollywood. "He got screwed royally," remarked the writer Harlan Ellison, a longtime Bloch friend. "There was never any attempt to cut him in, ever."

Bloch began his writing career as a teenager. He became a fan, and later a protégé, of H. P. Lovecraft (the author of such horror fiction classics as *The Dunwich Horror* and *The Shadow Out of Time*), and sold his first story, "The Secret in the Tomb," to *Weird Tales* magazine in 1933 for twenty dollars. The sale established what would become a long-standing relationship between Bloch and the "fantastic" pulp periodicals of the time: *Unknown Worlds, Marvel Tales, Fantastic Adventures,* and *The Mystery Companion* were magazines that dealt with tales of terror, the supernatural, and the just plain weird. In the forties, Bloch adapted thirty-nine of his stories for the radio series *Stay Tuned for Terror,* and his first novel, *The Scarf,* was published to good reviews in 1947. Twenty books followed, and of his four hundred short stories, "Yours Truly, Jack the Ripper" is the most famous.

The late fifties found Bloch, then in his early forties, living in the farm country of northern Wisconsin, a short distance from the nondescript town of Plainfield. And location, to borrow a tenet from the real estate profession, did indeed prove to be everything in relation to the birth of *Psycho.*

In the fall of 1957 Ed Gein, a fifty-one-year-old handyman, and one of Plainfield's most solitary citizens, was arrested on suspicion of having murdered Bernice Worden, a middle-aged merchant. With Gein in custody, local police officials conducted a search of his isolated, decrepit farmhouse, and in the process stumbled upon one of the ghastliest crime scenes in the country's history.

Bernice Worden's mutilated body was one of the first discoveries. Her nude, headless torso was found disemboweled and hanging from a makeshift pulley in the Gein parlor.

One grim revelation followed another. A wall of masks turned out to be human faces that had been peeled from skulls and preserved so skillfully that one was recognized as the visage of another middle-aged woman who had been missing for several years. A coffee can was found to contain the genitalia of several women, maintained crudely in rock salt, while a belt made entirely of female nipples was discovered hanging on a doorknob.

Gein soon confessed that in addition to murder, he had indulged in grave robbing as a means of obtaining his grisly souvenirs. He also admitted that he would, on occasion, don the skins of his victims and prance for hours around his deserted property late at night under the summer moon.

Details of Gein's ghoulish secret life appalled locals and soon became the focus of national media attention. Nearby resident Robert Bloch, fascinated by "the notion that the man next door may be a monster, unsuspected even in the gossip-ridden microcosm of small-town life," utilized Gein as a blueprint for the creation of *Psycho*'s murderous mama's boy, Norman Bates.

(Norman—or more specifically that part of him that became Mother—owes a small debt also to an earlier Bloch story, *The Real Bad Friend,* about a seemingly normal suburban man who takes on the personality of an imaginary pal in order to murder his wife.)

In Bloch's novel—as opposed to the film version—Norman Bates has several of the same characteristics as Ed Gein. Both are middle-aged loners who were mentally and emotionally warped by sex-hating, Bible-thumping, domineering mothers. Gein told authorities that he performed his atrocities while in a "blackout kind of daze," and Norman drinks himself into a similar state as a prelude to committing murder.

But the two men have their differences as well. While Gein's victims were older, mother-substitutes, Norman kills attractive young women. And Gein never preserved his mother's corpse.

In fact, the legend that he practiced taxidermy on his victims stems directly from the avocation of his fictional counterpart in *Psycho*. Ed Gein was, by any standards, a monstrous psychopath; one must look back to medieval times to find individual crimes as grotesque as his. By comparison, Norman Bates seems like a choirboy.

Along with the shocking human remains discovered at the Gein house were stacks of old periodicals dating back to the thirties. Among Ed's favorite reading subjects were lurid tales of the Nazi atrocities of World War II and tabloid accounts of the Christine Jorgensen sex-change scandal of 1952. Included in the Gein collection were *Unknown Worlds* and *Marvel Tales*, magazines containing stories by Robert Bloch that Ed must surely have read. "I never thought about that," Bloch said reflectively in 1994.

Hitchcock initially turned *Psycho* over to screenwriter James Cavanaugh, but the resulting script proved unsatisfactory. "It took some kind of genius," Peggy Robertson says, "to make that story dull, but Cavanaugh managed to do it!" When Joseph Stefano was brought into the project, Hitch knew he had found a scenarist who would be able to transform a good book into a brilliant screenplay.

In the fall of 1959—with Stefano's completed screenplay at his disposal—Hitchcock began firming up the other elements required to bring *Psycho* to the screen. It's been said that he was so concerned about keeping the story line of the movie a secret that he would refer to it publicly only as "Production #9401," but this is simply not the case. It's true that he wanted to keep the details of the plot and the actual filming as quiet as possible, but the title had been public knowledge from day one of preproduction, when the project was announced in the Hollywood industry trade papers. And anyone deeply interested in learning the basic story line had only to purchase the Bloch novel to do so. (In fact,

Five years before dressing up as Mother Bates, Tony Perkins donned comic drag for a farcical scene in The Matchmaker, *opposite Shirley Booth.*

months before filming began, Hitch received a letter from a fan inquiring as to what Mother's corpse was going to look like, as he wanted to duplicate her appearance for a Halloween party. Hitchcock patiently wrote back and stated that Mother's look hadn't been designed yet.)

To keep his production costs down, Hitchcock assembled a crew culled primarily from the capable staff of his television series, then in its fourth successful year. Hilton Green had worked often as the series' first assistant director, and he was pleased to assume the same position on *Psycho*.

"*North by Northwest* had been his highest budget to date," Green recalls, "and with *Psycho* he wanted to prove that he could make a low-budget, quality picture. He wanted to make good pictures without wasting money—and as we all know, there is a lot of waste in Hollywood. He really wanted to do something meaningful, in an inexpensive way, and *Psycho* was the perfect vehicle for that."

From his TV team, Hitch enlisted the services of cinematographer John L. Russell and set designer George Milo. For the all-important job of editing the film, he turned to George Tomasini. Gifted composer Bernard Herrmann, a longtime Hitchcock associate, was contracted to compose the picture's score, and Saul Bass was hired to design the striking opening titles and also to lay out the shower-murder sequence. Amazingly, all of this top talent was acquired for less than $62,000.

Hitchcock knew full well that by simply being associated with him, a craftsman or actor's career was enhanced, and this knowledge allowed him to sign some remarkable collaborators at rock-bottom prices.

Hitch's financial austerity program for *Psycho* extended, of course, to his cast of actors as well. Accustomed to receiving up to $100,000 for her services, Janet Leigh accepted just $25,000 to play Marion Crane in the film for which she is now most famous. "I would have done it for nothing," she admits today, "but my agents would have had heart attacks!" Janet's salary was based on the fact that she would be working on the picture for only three weeks out of the two-month shoot.

The highest acting fee went to Anthony Perkins, who was paid $40,000 to portray Norman Bates and Mother. John Gavin received $30,000 for six weeks' work as Marion's lover, Sam Loomis, while Vera Miles was contracted to receive $10,000 to play Marion's sister, Lila. Martin Balsam, a swarthy character actor, was signed to play the private detective known only as Arbogast for $6,000; and to portray the long-winded psychiatrist who explains Norman's mental condition in the film's denouement, Simon Oakland was hired for $1,000 for two days' work. Hitchcock's actress/daughter Patricia—who had appeared in her father's films *Stage Fright* and *Strangers on a Train,* as well as in several of his TV shows—received $500 for two days as Marion's coworker. One of the film's lowest salaries—$200— went to Ted Knight, later to win fame as Ted Baxter of *The Mary Tyler Moore Show,* who, in a nonspeaking role, played a police guard in one of *Psycho*'s final moments.

So, what caliber of talent did Hitch acquire with his skimpy budget? The two most crucial characters in the story, Marion and Norman, had been cast with actors who brought experience and box-office appeal to the picture. Anthony Perkins, at twenty-seven, had successfully played farce with Shirley MacLaine in *The Matchmaker* (Thornton Wilder's turn-of-the-century trifle that would later serve as the basis for *Hello, Dolly!*), and was equally effective as a sensitive romantic lead opposite Audrey Hepburn in *Green Mansions.* He gave strong dramatic performances in *On the Beach* and *Fear Strikes Out,* and was nominated for an Oscar as Best Supporting Actor of 1957 for his gripping portrayal of a young Quaker torn between traditional religious values and his desire to fight in the Civil War in *Friendly Persuasion.*

Lanky, and with dark good looks that could change light-

ninglike from brooding intensity to open, boyish charm, Perkins was also something of a teen heartthrob who had scored a top forty hit with "Moonlight Swim" (during an era when every potential young dreamboat was encouraged to cut records in the wake of Elvis Presley's astounding success).

Paul Jasmin, a lifelong friend of Perkins (and one of the voices of Mother in *Psycho*), recalls that his pal expressed no qualms about taking the part, one that he would be associated with for the rest of his career. "I just remember that he was so excited about working with Alfred Hitchcock," Jasmin says. "I think he thought it was a great challenge to work with him. He really *loved* Hitchcock. Later on in life, he used to joke about it because people identified him with *Psycho* so much, but at the time, I don't think he expressed any misgivings or reservations at all. Tony thought he was in the middle of making *the* career move of his life, and he was right."

Perkins did, however, feel he might face career repercussions as a result of playing such a bizarre, villainous role, and he shared his reservations with Hitchcock. "He agreed that it was a gamble," Perkins recalled years later. "He had no idea of the real possible success of the picture, but he suggested that I give it a try anyway."

John Gavin, a handsome, sturdily built actor of modest range, was being groomed by Universal to follow in the size-twelve footsteps of the studio's top star, Rock Hudson, whom Gavin strongly resembled. Some eyebrows were raised when Hitchcock cast Gavin as Sam, especially since the director had screened films of other, more compelling competitors for the role.

Brian Keith, Cliff Robertson, Leslie Nielsen, Richard Basehart, and Stuart Whitman were all in the running, but Gavin turned out to be the most cost-effective choice, and since Hitch felt that the parts of both Sam and Lila were merely "cardboard characters," he reasoned that the intensity of a Cliff Robertson or Stuart Whitman might distract audiences from the real stars of the story, Marion and Norman. And despite his reserved acting style, Gavin was sexy enough for filmgoers to understand Marion's attraction to him and the out-of-character robbery she performs in the hope of starting a life with him. Just prior to being cast in *Psycho,* Gavin had scored with female fans as the long-suffering love interest of Lana Turner in the hugely popular soap opera *Imitation of Life,* and it was hoped that some of that film's box-office magic would cling to Gavin for *Psycho.*

Financial considerations also accounted for Vera Miles's being given the part of Lila. Miles was under personal contract to Hitchcock, who had at first wanted to groom her into a replacement for his favorite leading lady of the fifties, Grace Kelly.

Kelly had excelled in her three Hitchcock-guided films, *Rear Window, Dial M for Murder,* and *To Catch a Thief,* and if she hadn't chosen marriage to a European prince over a movie career, Hitch would have been content to cast her in every movie he had on the planning boards. He was the first director to properly exploit Kelly's elegant sexuality for the camera, and he felt he could do the same for Vera Miles, an attractive young television actress he signed up shortly after Kelly's marriage to Prince Rainier in 1956. Miles had, in fact, starred in the premier episode of *Alfred Hitchcock Presents.*

But a year later, when Miles failed to generate much public interest opposite Henry Fonda in Hitchcock's near flop, *The Wrong Man,* and then declined the lead in *Vertigo* because of pregnancy, Hitch lost interest in promoting her. When the rather drab role of Lila Crane in *Psycho* came along, Hitchcock exercised his option on Vera's services, and gave her the part.

By the time Janet Leigh signed the contracts on October 28, 1959, to play the pivotal role of Marion Crane, she had starred in thirty-two films, in a wide variety of roles, and was thirty-two years old. Always self-effacing (you'll note she nearly always

refers to her director as Mr. Hitchcock in this text, a result perhaps of the respect she was taught as a youngster at MGM—a
habit shared by her peers June Allyson and Elizabeth Taylor),
Janet has often credited sheer good fortune for much of her success. While the element of luck and timing is essential to any successful show-business career, it was also her natural ability, great
looks, affinity with audiences, and enthusiastic willingness to
expand and test her talents that cemented her position as one of
the most popular leading ladies of the fifties and sixties.

There is, however, no denying the major role fate played in
her entree into the motion picture business. The story of her "discovery"—free of any hype or exaggeration—is one of the most
remarkable in the history of Tinseltown. It is, to quote Jack Lemmon's character in *Some Like It Hot,* "one for Ripley."

In February 1946, while vacationing at the Sugar Bowl Ski
Lodge, nestled in California's Sierra Nevada mountains, actress
Norma Shearer and her husband Marty Arrougé paused one
afternoon at the resort's registration desk, manned by Fred Morrison. Shearer, who was four years into retirement following a long
reign as the elegantly beautiful prima donna of Metro-Goldwyn-
Mayer, noticed a framed photograph of a smiling young woman
at Morrison's elbow.

"What a pretty face," Shearer remarked. "She should be in
pictures." Morrison proudly accepted the compliment on behalf
of his eighteen-year-old daughter, Jeanette, but he was taken
aback when Shearer added, "May I have a copy of that photo to
take with me?"

Several days later, when Shearer left the lodge to return to
Hollywood, Morrison made sure she was armed with the photo
she had admired and several other snapshots of Jeanette as well.
An avid movie fan, Jeanette was thrilled to hear of her father's
encounter with a glamorous star, but she had little hope that the
exchange of photos would lead to anything. Her life was rooted
firmly in working-class reality: She was newly married to a strug-

gling young musician, Stan Reames, and they were eking out a living in the industrial town of Stockton in central California.

Four months later, with the Shearer incident all but forgotten, the Reameses relocated to Los Angeles, where Stan hoped to establish himself as the leader of a dance band. While staying at a run-down hotel in a dreary section of Hollywood, Jeanette received a letter that had been forwarded from Stockton. It was from an agent, Levis Green, and it beckoned her to the Beverly Hills offices of the Music Corporation of America, the most prestigious talent agency in town.

At first, Jeanette thought there had been a mix-up, that the letter was intended for her husband. But she soon learned that Norma Shearer and Marty Arrougé had practically forced Jeanette's photographs on agent Charles Feldman and MGM executive Benny Thau over dinner one night at Chasen's restaurant in Beverly Hills. When MCA president Lew Wasserman and his wife Edie stopped by the table to say hello, Feldman and Thau—who weren't terribly impressed with the photos—saw an opportunity to placate Shearer and passed the shots along to Wasserman, who in turn handed them over to Levis Green, who *was* impressed enough to write to Jeanette at her Stockton address in order to set up an interview.

Within two days of her phone call to MCA in answer to the letter, Jeanette—wide-eyed and nervous—was ushered by Levis Green through the gates of the MGM lot in Culver City for the first time.

Although she had appeared in some minor college productions and on occasion sung with her husband's band, Jeanette had never seriously entertained any show-business aspirations. Yet here she was, being given the once-over by studio personnel, who very much liked what they saw: honey-blond hair framing a lovely face dominated by intelligent, doelike eyes and shaped by bone structure that would clearly be camera-friendly, and below this a sexy figure that was buxom yet fashionably svelte.

Her looks alone augured well for starlet potential, but what surprised and delighted Lillian Burns Sidney (MGM's influential maven of talent development) was the discovery of Jeanette's innate acting ability and a bright, sincere personality that seemed tailor-made for the movies. To Jeanette's utter astonishment, she was immediately signed to a seven-year contract that would, at first, pay her a then-handsome fifty dollars a week. The studio, per its normal policy, held the option of letting her go after three months, and Jeanette was convinced it would do just that.

"I gave her a tender farewell scene to memorize from *Thirty Seconds Over Tokyo*," Sidney recalls. "And as nervous and excited as she was, she came back two days later and read the scene better than Phyllis Thaxter had in the movie!" (Janet points to luck again for this break, as she had seen the film more than once, and remembered the scene vividly.)

Just days later, Lillian Burns Sidney summoned Jeanette back to the studio to meet with producer Jack Cummings and director Roy Rowland, who were preparing a new Van Johnson vehicle, *The Romance of Rosy Ridge,* set in the post–Civil War era. The two men told Jeanette that Mrs. Sidney had been so impressed with her that they were willing to take a whopping chance and have Jeanette screen-tested for the female lead in their picture. She would be auditioning for the role of Lissy Anne, a naive young mountain girl and Van Johnson's love interest. This despite the fact that Beverly Tyler, an up-and-coming actress with three good pictures behind her—and a boyfriend in the higher echelon of MGM—was all but set for the part. "The first day I was at the studio," Janet recalls, "I was sitting in Miss Burns's office (I always called Lillian Burns Sidney 'Miss Burns') when Beverly Tyler came in wearing a period costume on the day *she* was testing for Lissy Anne. I was thrilled to see a face I recognized from the movies."

Despite her nerves and inexperience, Jeanette found to her great relief that once she donned the old-fashioned dress and hairstyle of the character, she began to identify with Lissy Anne, and the scene became real to her. "I felt Jeanette slipping away and Lissy Anne emerging," she recalls. Cummings, Rowland, and Van Johnson were delighted with the test, but Tyler was still very much in the running for the role as well. The following Saturday, all three men ran Jeanette's and Tyler's tests in the presence of Louis B. Mayer, the studio's all-powerful chief. Following the screening, Mayer thought for a moment and then announced with certainty, "The new one is perfect for the role. We gamble and go with her. A star is born."

So, within weeks of her first visit to a studio lot, and with no prior dreams of an acting career, Jeanette was under contract to the greatest film studio in the world, would soon be starring in a movie opposite Van Johnson, the premier heartthrob of the day, and had even been given a new name, Janet Leigh, conjured up by Johnson himself. When Norma Shearer, still highly prized by MGM as the widow of beloved producer Irving Thalberg, showed up one afternoon to pose for publicity photos with Johnson and her new discovery, Janet felt a strong sense of unreality about it all, as if she were living out the climax of an elaborate, completely unbelievable dream.

Though it wasn't a dream, it *was* unbelievable, even by Hollywood's hyperbolic standards. When Janet sat down to be profiled for the first time by the studio publicity department, she told them how she came to be put under contract. "That's a wonderful story!" they marveled. "We couldn't have thought of a better one ourselves. But you should tell us how it *really* happened, so we can be prepared."

Given this amazing opportunity, Janet plunged into her new occupation with customary energy, enthusiasm, and concentration. "Janet has this well of spirit or charisma or whatever you want to call it," Lillian Sidney says, "that comes out and grabs you. And at the beginning of her career, all she lacked was experience. But I have to say, nobody worked harder or learned more—and faster—than Janet did." (Janet was so inexperienced in the ways of Hollywood that during preproduction of *Rosy Ridge,* she tearfully announced that she would have to drop out of the picture because she couldn't afford to pay for the train trip and hotel accommodations required for location shooting.)

When *The Romance of Rosy Ridge* was released in 1947, Janet Leigh was hailed as "a piquant new discovery," and her career was launched. She spent the next decade avoiding typecasting in a string of popular films. Sweetly charming in *Little Women* and *Words and Music,* she was no less effective in the romantic dramas *The Red Danube* and *Holiday Affair*, the latter becoming a perennial Christmas season favorite on TV.

A resilient Western heroine in *The Naked Spur,* she proved to be a deft comedienne in *The Perfect Furlough* and *Who Was That Lady?* Luscious in such color escapist fare as *Scaramouche, Prince Valiant,* and *Houdini,* she was believable as well in the African wilds of *Safari.*

My Sister Eileen, Walking My Baby Back Home, and *Two Tickets to Broadway* allowed her to display graceful dancing and singing talents, and she even suffered the perils of film noir in the highly regarded *Act of Violence.* Her costars during these years included Ethel Barrymore, John Wayne, Jack Lemmon, James Stewart, Robert Mitchum, Robert Wagner, Elizabeth Taylor, Dean Martin and Jerry Lewis, and—in six films—the startlingly handsome Tony Curtis, who became her husband in a highly publicized 1951 union. (Janet's marriage to Stan Reames had dissolved just as her acting career was taking off.)

"I think my parents, because of their great beauty," says actress Jamie Lee Curtis, "were not accepted for their serious work as quickly and effusively as other actors."

It's true that Janet's loveliness probably kept her from being cast in some choice, earthy roles that went to plainer, Method-trained actresses, but she could always be counted on to make the absolute most of any acting challenge presented to her.

There's no doubt that Alfred Hitchcock saw her striking performance as a terrified young bride in Orson Welles's classic drama of the Tijuana underworld, *Touch of Evil.* Filmed in black and white, the film went into release just a year before the *Psycho* casting process got under way.

Also, Hitch would sometimes socialize with the Curtises, and, knowing what an analytical mind he possessed, it's not a stretch to imagine that during such occasions he took the opportunity to study Janet's singular qualities, possibly with an eye to casting her specifically as Marion Crane, or possibly considering her for future roles.

By signing Janet for *Psycho*, Hitchcock got quite a bit more than just an experienced actress whom he could trust to bring her character compellingly to life. He also acquired a big star, whose sudden, shocking demise early in the film would stun and confuse audiences. And Janet was not just any star, but one filmgoers really admired—both as a dependable performer and as a famous wife and mother. The warm regard in which the public held Janet would add an element of pathos to the savage killing of Marion Crane that would be largely absent if the role were played by an actress with a less sympathetic public persona.

With his cast and crew in place, and after all was said and done, the final *Psycho* preproduction and shooting budget totaled an astonishingly low $806,947.55, a figure that wouldn't come close to covering the costs of a short film in the cost-inflated Hollywood of today. But in spite of the meager budget, Paramount would only agree to distribute and promote *Psycho* if Hitchcock agreed to finance the picture himself through his Shamley Productions. The studio had grave misgivings about the project, which it considered vulgar and a probable magnet for censorship headaches. It had been, after all, a Paramount reader who labeled the property "impossible for films," in the first place. The studio's top production executives had hoped that his next film, which would amount to their final commitment from Hitchcock, would be a lushly produced, elegant mystery with top stars filmed in sparkling color, in the tradition of the director's prior hits for the studio, *Rear Window* and *The Man Who Knew Too Much.*

But Hitch, like any great artist, wasn't interested in repeating his past glories; he looked instead to new creative challenges—and a wider profit margin.

Financial considerations aside, what were the elements in *Psycho* that appealed to Alfred Hitchcock, the world-class filmmaker? "Hitch was fascinated by the idea that the story starts out as one thing—Marion's dilemma—then, after a horrible murder, turns into something else," recalls Hitchcock associate Ned Brown.

Yet when asked by French director François Truffaut why he chose to make the film, Hitchcock replied, "I think the thing that appealed to me was the suddenness of the murder in the shower, coming, as it were, out of the blue. That was about all."

There was another motivation, however, that Hitch kept to himself. In the midfifties, Truffaut's countryman, Henri-Georges Clouzot—fresh from the international triumph of *The Wages of Fear*—directed Simone Signoret in *Diabolique,* a low-budget, black-and-white murder mystery with a heart-stopping surprise ending (which took place in a white-tiled bathroom.) The film was immediately hailed as a classic of the genre, and Clouzot was tagged "the French Hitchcock."

With *Psycho,* Hitch was determined that if anyone— whether a Hollywood schlockmeister who specialized in cheap horror flicks, or an award-winning European director—was going to try and outdo him, the master would have the last laugh and succeed the most brilliantly.

A month before Janet set foot on the *Psycho* set for the first time, on November 30, 1959, much of the location footage that would provide the visual backdrop for her performance had already been shot.

In October, Hitchcock dispatched assistant director Hilton Green and a small production team to Phoenix to capture *Psycho*'s opening moments and to research locations that would be re-created back at the Revue Productions soundstages on the lot of Universal Studios in the San Fernando Valley.

"For the picture's first scene," Green recalled, "Hitch wanted a helicopter shot coming in over the Phoenix skyline, and then slowly going over to the hotel [where Marion and Sam are concluding their noontime tryst], and finally coming in through the actual hotel window and settling on John Gavin and Janet in bed. But we couldn't get it. That was several years before the real solid [camera] mounts were developed, and it was just too shaky."

For the finished film, it became necessary for editor George Tomasini to splice the aerial footage into a studio close-up of a mock hotel window. Perfectionist Hitchcock was never satisfied with the results, and indeed, keen observers can point out the difference between the film shot by helicopter in Arizona and the soundstage footage of the hotel window.

While in Phoenix, Green also took still photos of various locations—from a list of 140 suggested locales that had been scouted earlier—that could be constructed on the Universal lot. Hitch wanted Marion Crane's everyday world, and the general ambience of the Phoenix business district, to be realized on film with precise authenticity. "He gave me a Polaroid Land camera," Green says. "They had just come out and were big stuff. We shot numerous real estate offices, of the type where Marion would have worked, and the kind of middle-class homes that she and her sister would have lived in. I came back to Hollywood raving about the camera, because I could see what I had shot immediately." (Hitchcock was so grateful for Green's contributions to the look of *Psycho*'s Phoenix scenes that he gifted him with a Polaroid camera at the conclu-

sion of filming, a rare gesture of generosity from the director.)

Hitch's exacting specifications surprised Helen Colvig, the film's wardrobe supervisor. "His research was so pure," she remembered. "He laid out photographs for every major character. In Phoenix, he'd found a girl like Marion, gone into her home, and [had Hilton Green] photograph everything from her closet, her bureau drawers, her suitcases."

(Norman Bates's natural habitat was also based on an actual location. Hitchcock had photographs taken of a slightly run-down Victorian mansion in Kent, Ohio, near the Kent State campus, to serve as the basis for the design and construction of the forbidding house on the hill that sheltered Norman and Mother Bates. In the 1960s and 1970s, the prototype of the Bates mansion in Kent was home to such social and political groups as the controversial Students for a Democratic Society.)

Another camera crew was sent up to Highway 99 between the cities of Fresno and Bakersfield in California's central valley to shoot day and night film of the road that would later be rear-projected behind Janet as she "drove" Marion's car in her flight from Phoenix. Also put on film were the location shots necessary for a memorable scene in which Marion is questioned by a suspicious highway patrolman.

Hitchcock's careful attention to detail in the preproduction phase of *Psycho* was tremendously helpful to Janet. She was ultimately required to appear at only one location shoot (not that she would have objected to attending others), but more important, his extensive research in Phoenix helped her as an actor to gain insight into Marion Crane's life and surroundings. By typically leaving little to chance in his preplanning, Hitch had created a polished setting for the multifaceted jewel that Janet's performance would become.

Christopher Nickens

1959

Another year of general euphoria. More Americans than ever had the time and money to pursue such innocent pastimes as boating and the lively arts. Alaska and Hawaii achieved statehood. The space program was accelerating. Oklahoma repealed Prohibition, leaving Mississippi as the only dry state.

Nikita Khrushchev and Vice President Richard M. Nixon tangled in the famous "kitchen debate," and Khrushchev toured the United States. The world was introduced to new global figures like John F. Kennedy and Fidel Castro while old heroes like Errol Flynn and Winston Churchill were given grand farewells.

We were singing "Climb Ev'ry Mountain" and "The Sound of Music," and seeing *Some Like It Hot* and *North by Northwest*. *Gypsy* and *The Miracle Worker* were on Broadway stages and Michener's *Hawaii* and Drury's *Advise and Consent* were on bedside tables from coast to coast.

Garbo slouch hats, loose-fitting sweaters, and Barbie dolls were "in."

And in October of 1959, Alfred Hitchcock sent me a novel by Robert Bloch entitled *Psycho*, which was to be Mr. Hitchcock's next film. The role he was offering me was that of Mary Crane— and it was destined to affect my life from that moment on.

At that time, I was Mrs. Tony Curtis and had been since 1951. We had two beautiful daughters, Kelly Lee and Jamie Lee.

The marriage was functioning fairly well, just the usual run-of-the-mill spats. All in all, our lives were in a very good place.

Both of our careers were in high gear. Tony had received an Oscar nomination for *The Defiant Ones; Some Like It Hot* had been released in the summer to raves; and he'd finished *Operation Petticoat* in the spring.

Together, Tony and I had completed *The Vikings* and *The Perfect Furlough*. And then we had delivered our own production—a second baby—at the end of 1958. A year later, in August 1959, we'd finished *Who Was That Lady?*

Our personal "Tinseltown Trolley" was merrily tooting along. We moved in privileged circles. We saw the latest movies at various private projection rooms. We played team gin rummy with Anne and Kirk Douglas, Edie Adams and Ernie Kovacs, Gloria and Sammy Cahn, Audrey and Billy Wilder. We attended intimate dinners and big soirees at Irving "Swifty" Lazar's, Frank Sinatra's, Edie and Lew Wasserman's, Jeanne and Dean Martin's, Pat Kennedy and Peter Lawford's. We moved into a larger home in Beverly Hills with a cook, two nannies, two maids, and a secretary. We bought another house in Palm Springs. We drove a Rolls-Royce and a Lincoln Continental, and kept a station wagon for household needs. We entertained. Heady stuff.

We had met Alma and Alfred Hitchcock socially a few years back—at the Wassermans' and the Tom Mays' and at various special events. The four of us were not bosom buddies, but we always enjoyed their company, and particularly Mr. Hitchcock's famous wit.

This is out of context, I realize, but I can't resist telling this story here. In August of 1974, Hitch's seventy-fifth birthday, there was a huge celebration at Chasen's, a chic Beverly Hills restaurant, with a receiving line, klieg lights, red carpet, extensive media coverage, and all the other fancy trimmings. Anyone who was anyone in the industry was there. By now I was Mrs.

Robert Brandt and when Hitch saw Bob and me coming through the line, he motioned for us to step closer to him, and while cameras were rolling and people were waiting in the line, he whispered in our ears the naughtiest story I have ever heard. He was such a lovable rascal!

Another quick Hitchcockism! When he was finally knighted, there was a luncheon and press conference at Universal Studios. Cary Grant and I were among those attending. When asked why the queen had waited so long to recognize him, he replied, "I guess she forgot."

By October 1959, Tony and I had seen almost every Alfred Hitchcock movie made, and many of his TV shows. We were serious fans and had profound respect for his talent. Therefore, I was thrilled that I was being offered a role in an Alfred Hitchcock film.

I eagerly ripped open the manila envelope that housed the medium-size book the messenger had delivered from my agents at MCA. An attached note read something like this:

Please consider the part of Mary. In the
completed script Mary will be improved upon
and, of course, the descriptions of the
characters will be completely different.
Anthony Perkins is set to play Norman Bates.

I read the novel in one sitting. Mesmerized. It was not a pretty picture Mr. Bloch had word-painted. In fact, it was downright ugly and frightening.

Quite frankly, I had not read the novel since that initial introduction. In preparation for this undertaking, I hustled to my library to reread, to jolt my memory into re-creating that first powerful impression. Alas, it was nowhere to be found. Someone had obviously "borrowed" it—permanently. Collectors Book Store in Hollywood had two signed paperback editions, which now boasted a cover shot of me screaming. The going rate for one copy was fifty dollars. Can you imagine what the copy Hitchcock sent me would be worth today?!

To synopsize: The text begins with a fat, balding, alcoholic motel proprietor (Norman Bates), who is burdened with his obsessive, domineering, demented mother, in an antiquated, forbidding house with six unattached cabins, situated in an isolated, dreary locale. We quickly learn that Norman's hobbies are taxidermy, quirky psychology, and occultism. Mother's only hobby is tormenting Norman.

Enter Mary Crane. Late twenties. Mildly attractive. But drawn and nervous. No wonder—she has just stolen $40,000 from the real estate office where she works. She isn't a thief by trade, but she is desperately trying to build a life for herself with the man she loves, who is debt-ridden and, therefore, unable or unwilling to marry. This is her last chance to grab the brass ring of happiness.

She is fleeing to her lover (Sam Loomis), but she is exhausted, and takes a wrong turn in stormy weather. The Bates Motel sign is a beckoning haven.

In answer to Mary's ringing, Norman finally shuffles to the motel office and shows her to the first adjoining cabin. When she asks about a diner, he suggests that she share his supper at the house because the nearest restaurant is far away. During the meal, he discloses the tense situation with his mother, and in the course of sympathizing with Norman's predicament, Mary realizes she is setting herself up for an even worse entrapment than his by taking the money from her employer.

She returns to her room, having decided to drive the long road home and give back the money. Feeling good about her resolution, she decides to take a shower to cleanse her outer self as she has her inner self. And a crazy old lady with a knife kills her.

Earlier, Norman had escorted Mary back to the cabin, then retreated to his office—where he's stashed his liquor, because Mother doesn't want him to drink—and proceeds to get sloshed. But, before he passes out, he manages to stagger to his secret peephole behind a framed license on the wall to watch the girl undress.

When he comes to, he hears the roaring sound of water and goes to explore the source. He discovers the grisly corpse, and knows what he has to do. He has to protect Mother. He cleans up the mess, puts everything in the girl's car, and sinks it in a nearby swamp.

Sam Loomis, the man Mary loves, receives a visit from Mary's sister, Lila Crane, and a private insurance investigator, Milton Arbogast. Both suspect Sam of being Mary's accomplice in the robbery. When he convinces them that he knows nothing, the three become really concerned—where is Mary! Arbogast has found that the trail leads to the Bates Motel. He questions Norman, who avoids answering, but when Arbogast insists on interviewing the woman he has seen peering from the upstairs window, Norman has to acquiesce. However, he insists that he has to alert Mother that a visitor is coming.

After a few moments, Arbogast follows Norman to the house. Mother opens the door and welcomes Arbogast by slashing him to pieces with a straight razor.

Once again, Norman's job is to clear out any trace of

Mother's lapses. Only this time he firmly insists that she hide in the fruit cellar because there will surely be others coming to inquire about the missing detective and the girl.

Norman, of course, is right. It isn't long before Sam and Lila pick up Arbogast's lead and arrive at the motel. Lila notices Mary's handwriting on the registration ledger, and noting that she had stayed in cabin six, declares six to be their lucky number and the cabin in which they wish to stay. Norman isn't fooled, but he doesn't argue; after all, he'll be able to keep tabs on these intruders through his peep hole.

Norman watches the couple rummage through the bedroom and then the bathroom. He sees Lila find Mary's earring behind the toilet bowl. Norman hears their plan—she'll go for the sheriff while he engages Mr. Bates in conversation until she returns. Norman hears the car drive away and sees Sam approaching the office. Norman also sees the car stop. Although he is quite drunk, he is still very shrewd—he knows the girl is going to try to find Mother.

After offering Sam a drink, Norman explains how he has kept Mother alive when everyone else has thought she was dead, how he has just seen Sam's car stop and how he has to defend Mother against all strangers. Suddenly he hits Sam over the head with the liquor bottle and scurries to the main house.

Meanwhile Lila has slipped around the back of the motel and makes her way to the old house. When no one answers her knock, she tries a skeleton key she has in her purse and it works. She searches throughout the creaky, decrepit place, and finally ends up in the cellar. There she finds the inner fruit cellar, where a figure sits in a rocker. She turns the chair and sees a sunken, leathery face staring at her, and then hears clattering steps coming down the stairs. She gasps in horror at the grotesque shape of a costumed, painted Norman Bates lunging at her with a knife. She screams as Sam comes running to subdue the hysterical woman who is Norman Bates.

Later, Sam explains to Lila that the psychiatrists on the case have reported the following conclusions: Norman Bates had a strong relationship with his mother and they felt he was secretly a transvestite before Mrs. Bates died. Her husband had run off, causing Mrs. Bates to hate men and dominate her already weak son. Along came Joe Considine, who courted her and persuaded her to sell the family farm and buy the motel. When Norman surprised his mother and her suitor in bed it sent him off the deep end. He poisoned them both with strychnine, then faked a suicide note. But later he realized that he wanted her back, so part of Norman *became* his mother. He dug her up, preserved her, and the three of them lived together: Norman as the little boy reigned over by Mother; Norman as Mother, who chastised her gutless son; and Norman as the man who took care of Mother.

And in the end, Mother has won out over all three!

I just sat—stunned. It was tantalizingly written. Horrific, sad, exciting. I tingled in anticipation of what "the Master of Suspense" would do with this material. He had already changed the unappealing profile of Norman Bates to the remarkably charming and charismatic conformation of Anthony Perkins. I couldn't wait to see what the talent of Perkins would bring to Norman and what other surprises the genius of Mr. Hitchcock had in store for me. For all of us. Because there was no doubt in my mind that I wanted to play Mary Crane. No doubt at all. I leaned over, quickly dialed MCA, and said yes. I didn't even ask what the salary was.

Ever since 1960, I have been asked many questions about Psycho. *We will answer those questions in this book as the story unfolds. Now is an appropriate time for the most frequently asked question:*

Was I the first choice to play Marion Crane?

I didn't know the answer to that until we started the research for this project. Because it never mattered to me if I had been the hundredth choice—I would have been grateful had the other ninety-nine turned it down.

So, I called upon the man who would know, Lew Wasserman, chairman of the board of MCA/Universal. He was president of MCA in 1959 and quite close to the Hitchcocks. Lew seldom, if ever, gives interviews, but because of our close relationship, he relented. (Edie and Lew Wasserman were among those responsible for my presence in Hollywood from day one. They are also godparents to my daughter Jamie Lee, and loyal, true friends.) He told me I was the first actress to be sent the novel with a definite offer. I felt really honored.

To be completely thorough, we also checked with Joseph Stefano, who wrote the brilliant screenplay of Psycho *and he confirmed Lew's opinion, as did Peggy Robertson, Mr. Hitchcock's personal assistant for many years. "It was always my understanding that Janet was going to do the picture," Ms. Robertson said. Of course, many people had been discussed for the role. Every talent agency in town had sent their client list to the office, hoping to fill any of the roles by sparking an interest from Mr. Hitchcock. But lucky me got the nod for Mary.*

When the real script finally arrived, I was full of expectation, salivating to partake of the delicacies sure to be offered from those pages. I was not disappointed.

A memo on the title page informed me that Mary Crane was now Marion Crane. The legal department had found an actual Mary Crane in the Phoenix telephone directory.

But that wasn't the only change. The script opened with a helicopter shot panning Phoenix, ending at a window in a sleazy hotel. Going into the murky room we see Marion Crane, attractive, in her late twenties, wearing a slip and relaxing on a mussed bed, but revealing an inner tension.

Standing over her is a handsome, bare-chested man, Sam

Loomis, her lover. He leans to embrace her, and she pulls him to her for a lingering kiss. Then Marion pulls away unwillingly and starts to dress. As she does, she tells Sam she cannot continue to live the way they have been existing. He counters that he has no choice—he's sick of paying his departed father's debts and his ex-wife's alimony, but what can he do.

Marion returns to the real estate office where she works to find that her boss has completed a cash deal with a rich, rude oilman, who attempts to pick up Marion. The employer asks Marion to deposit the money—$40,000—in the bank on her way home. She has always been a totally honest woman, but the temptation is just too great. She sees this money as the answer to her problems.

After trading in her car to throw a suspicious policeman off her trail, she embarks on the long ride to Sam. A torrential rainstorm causes her to miss the main highway, and she decides to stop at some forsaken motel. The young owner, Norman Bates, befriends her, and while she sits in the little parlor behind the motel office eating the simple meal he has prepared, he tells her he lives in that forbidding Victorian house up the hill in back with his domineering mother, whom he describes as mentally unbalanced. As she listens to Norman's tale of ensnarement, she realizes that because of her actions she is also trapped, and she resolves to return to Phoenix the next morning and face the consequences.

While Marion enjoys a shower, Norman seizes the opportunity to use his favorite vantage point, a peephole behind a picture on the wall in the small room adjoining cabin one, where Marion is staying. He is the voyeur for a bit, then quickly turns away and goes toward the main house, determined to have it out with Mother. Once there, however, he crumbles, and meekly sits in the dim kitchen, staring into space.

Mother, in shadow, enters the bathroom and stabs a screaming Marion to death. Minutes later, Norman appears and, though horrified, meticulously wipes away all evidence of the murder, depositing the body and Marion's possessions—including the stolen money, which had been wrapped in a newspaper—in her car, then sinking it all in a nearby swamp. He knows he has to take care of Mother.

The auto sinking is on page fifty-seven of the script. The last shot of the body wrapped up is on page fifty-five. The last shot of Marion's corpse is on page fifty-three.

I think a major clue, among many others of course, as to why Psycho *worked—meaning why it grabbed the audience at first and why it still does today—comes right at the beginning.*

When I recently spoke to Joseph Stefano, I asked him how he became associated with the project and who had come up with the concept for the opening.

This is Joseph Stefano's story: "Mr. Hitchcock was not happy with the first draft of Psycho. It bogged down, reducing it to a TV short horror story, rather than the classier feature he had hoped for. He also wasn't anxious to give me a hearing. Mr. H. did not relish working with people he didn't know; he felt comfortable with the tried and true. But local MCA agents, and finally a New York MCA agent, Kay Brown, persisted, and he agreed to see me to get them off his back.*

"When I read the book, I was immediately thrust into Norman Bates's world, and I didn't like Norman. I didn't particularly want to do a movie with a murder in it, either, especially the murder of someone no one knew very much about. After all, I had only done one film before this. But Mr. Hitchcock was one of the gifted directors I knew I could learn from. So I thought, 'There has to be a way to make this important.' Because I was beginning to feel that way about life—that people were getting murdered and we weren't much caring anymore. So, on the way to Paramount Studios for my meeting, I came up with the approach to suggest to Mr. Hitchcock: 'I see a movie about a young woman who is in a very difficult position—she is in love

with a young man who can't marry her. Here are two attractive people in a kind of hell of their own. And they are shacking up in a hotel room on her lunch hour.'

"Hitch's eyes lighted up; he loved that kind of thing.

"'There's only one problem: She doesn't want to do this anymore, so she puts her cards on the table and says they have to get married.'

"And I went on and on, describing what happens, how she has this moment when she digs her own trap. I built it right up to where she goes to the motel, meets Norman, sees her mistake, and gets killed.

"I didn't know if I had blown my chance with Mr. Hitchcock or not. But he leaned forward and said gleefully, 'We'll get a star to play the girl.'"

You see, what struck me when I read the script was—I really *cared* about Marion Crane, and that made all the difference. She was shown to us from page one; I knew her. I agonized with her over her troubles, I saw her in her house with her intimate things, I could see she was a decent person. I liked her. So, when she is killed, I was devastated.

And the fact that Norman is so appealing fuels the bewitching of the audience. There is a hint, a fleeting promise, that perhaps these two sorrowful souls might find solace with each other—an additional plunge for the audience's emotional roller coaster.

Joseph Stefano continued: "Hitchcock asked me why I didn't like Norman Bates [in the novel]. I said, 'Well, he's not sympathetic. He's unattractive; he drinks.' And Hitch asked, 'How would you feel about Tony Perkins?'

"I jumped at that. 'Oh, right! That's what I'm talking about.' I didn't know I wanted Tony Perkins, I just knew I wanted a sympathetic man."

Since Mr. Stefano and I were on the subject of casting, I

brought up an attributed quote of his from another earlier book on *Psycho*, in which he supposedly said that Mr. Hitchcock, in a formative session, was talking about an actress "much bigger" than Janet Leigh for Marion, but that Stefano didn't think she was very good.

Joseph Stefano: "Whoever she was, and I truly don't remember, I was referring to her body size, not name value. I believed if Marion was a large person, we would lose her vulnerability; she wouldn't be as effective as a victim. You do have to watch how you phrase remarks, don't you."

To return to the script outline. Three people undertake a search for the missing woman: her sister Lila, Sam, and an insurance detective known as Arbogast, who has been assigned to find the money. Arbogast's investigation leads him to the motel, where Norman refuses to allow him to question Mother. The detective calls Sam and Lila to tell them he found Norman's responses suspicious, then steals into the looming, rickety house to speak to the old lady. He makes his way into the musty foyer and up the stairs, but as he reaches the landing, he is swooped upon by Mrs. Bates, and he too is stabbed to death.

Lila and Sam now learn from the local sheriff that Norman Bates's mother has been dead and buried for the past eight years. They go to the motel, where they find evidence that Marion had indeed been there. Sam distracts Norman to allow Lila a chance to search the house. She is horrified when she discovers Mother's obscenely preserved corpse in the fruit cellar. Then she narrowly escapes death at the hands of a knife-wielding Norman, clothed as Mother. Sam rushes in and subdues the crazed man, who is later revealed by a doctor as a psychopathic transvestite who would assume his dead mother's personality, dress in her clothes, and kill young women who attracted him. In the end, Mother absorbs Norman totally.

I was intrigued with the alterations made by Mr. Stefano from the Bloch novel. In addition to witty, discerning dialogue, Stefano delivered an optical gem. For instance, he substituted a shred of torn paper in the toilet bowl for the lost earring behind the tank.

Joseph Stefano: "Because it was the first time a flushing toilet had ever been seen. *It was so* visual. *I fought very hard [with the censor's office] for the toilet and the word 'transvestite,' because they were so necessary. They questioned some of the strangest things. Like Janet's line in the opening scene, 'I'll lick the stamps.' I was furious. I said, 'Are you kidding? That defines the whole concept. What are you talking about? She's saying that she'll do anything, that she's desperate. What do* you *think she's saying?' And they did back off after that!"*

The next noticeable difference for me was the Arbogast murder. Instead of Mother meeting him at the front door, we see Arbogast cautiously slip in the door, stealthily creep up the stairs—the suspense mounting with each step—until at the top Mother comes screeching toward him and we see the weapon going up and down and Arbogast tumbling backward to the entry hall.

Joseph Stefano: "I did not know a great deal about camera angles yet, but I did know that Mr. Hitchcock knew everything. I spoke to him about moving the Arbogast murder so it would give him more options for his camera. Eventually we settled for the stairwell."

Mr. Bloch's book hinted at a budding romance between Lila and Sam. I preferred Stefano's script version, in which they just develop a friendly relationship. I thought somehow anything else would have cheapened their characters and the movie would have suffered.

In the book, Norman's condition is explained through Sam and Lila.

Joseph Stefano: "It was boring to have Sam and Lila driving along saying, 'Well, maybe it was because of this or maybe it was because of that.' I said, 'Let's get a psychiatrist in there and lay it out so everyone understands.'

"*I never believed it would be a hat grabber. Because by this time, we would need to know the* why *of Norman.*

"*It was thrilling for me at that early stage of my career as a writer to see someone of Mr. Hitchcock's stature be open and secure enough to accept a different approach. His mind was so quick to grasp the intent, to see the possibilities bloom.*"

I was really pumped up, I couldn't wait to start shooting. A few doubters voiced objections when they heard I would only appear in a smidge under forty percent of the picture. My retort was to cite the English thespians' attitude. You would see some of the biggest stars in England make a cameo appearance in a film. Obviously, their tenet was: It is the quality of the pages, not the quantity, that matters. What was good enough for Sir Ralph Richardson and Sir Laurence Olivier was certainly good enough for Janet Leigh.

PREPRODUCTION

The long-awaited day came—I was to meet Mr. Hitchcock at his home on Bellagio Road for a conference. On top of the desk in his study was a scaled model of every set to be used, complete with miniature furniture, breakaway walls, little dolls for people. This is where he planned every angle of his camera for each scene. He took great delight in showing me how my movement on a certain word would lead his camera to John Gavin (for example) and a two shot to heighten the drama of the moment.

In essence he explained: "I learned a long time ago—the hard way, I might add—never give the producer and editor too much footage to work with. They then have the capability to alter the thrust of a scene, even determine a performance, by snipping here or lengthening there. There is very little cutting needed on my films. I do as much as possible on the set with my camera."

Mr. Hilton Green was first assistant director on Psycho *and subsequently the producer on the sequels. He was also the "first" on many of the* Alfred Hitchcock Presents *television segments. He recalled that Mr. Hitchcock would sometimes cut after only a few lines of dialogue on a close-up, and the actor would worriedly ask what he had done wrong. But Mr. Hitchcock would say, "You were fine, that's a print. I only need the close shot for one line."*

Mr. Hitchcock continued: "I hired you because you are a talented actress. You are free to do whatever you wish with the role of Marion. I won't interfere unless you are having trouble and require my guidance. Or, if you are taking too big a slice of my pie [overacting] or if you are not taking enough of a slice of my pie. But there is one rule on the set—my camera is absolute. I tell the story through that lens, so I need you to move when my camera moves, stop when my camera stops. I'm confident you'll be able to find your motivation to justify the motion. Should you have difficulty, however, I will be happy to work with you. But I will not change the timing of my camera."

I have heard some performers express their unhappiness over Mr. Hitchcock's rigidness, they felt it was too restrictive. It really didn't disturb me that much. My impulse might have been to jump up earlier or later than he wanted, but it was only a question of rethinking and adjusting. Certainly no one could argue with his results. My motto was: Don't try to fix it if it ain't broke!

Apropos of my visit to Mr. Hitchcock's office, years later Tony Perkins and I were guests on The Dick Cavett Show *in New York; it may have been at the time of the* Psycho *rerelease in 1969. Anyway, when I mentioned this preshoot meeting with Hitch Tony's eyebrows shot up, and he asked, "Oh really? I never had any private discussions. But then I'm not a girl, or a blond." Of course, Dick Cavett had that same wicked sense of humor, and the two of them were unmerciful in their teasing. The more I explained, the deeper my foot went in my mouth. They were so wonderfully bad.*

Soon after our initial meeting in 1959, Mr. Hitchcock and I went to an optometrist. Hitch wanted the doctor to fit me with some contact lenses to wear for the close-up of the "dead" eyes. Unfortunately, the technique wasn't perfected then as it is now, and it would have taken six weeks for my eyes to accept those intruders without causing permanent damage. But we didn't have six weeks. So Hitch turned to me and said, "I guess you'll have to go it alone, ol' girl."

Next on the agenda were the wardrobe discussions. Helen Colvig was the designer for the film and Rita Riggs, a member of Mr. Hitchcock's regular television crew, was the on-the-set costumer. *Psycho* was her first feature film.

It was the practice at that time for the wardrobe to be custom-made, but Mr. Hitchcock insisted we shop in a regular ready-to-wear store. He asked us to buy Marion's two dresses off the rack and only pay what a secretary could afford. We all agreed.

Rita and I went to JAX, a then-popular boutique in Beverly Hills, and found two simple, solid-colored, shirtwaisted dresses. One was an off-white cotton, the other a blue wool jersey.

Rita commented, "Mr. Hitchcock likes good wool jersey; it reads well in black and white."

It was at that moment I realized that the picture was to be shot in black and white. I had been so captivated by the entire project that it hadn't occurred to me to even ask, such was the potency and power of Alfred Hitchcock.

Of course it had to be in black and white. Color would have ruined the darkness of the mood, even trivialized the contents. And the vivid red blood would have been too much for the censors.

The slip mentioned in the novel and script became a bra and a half-slip. For the opening love scene, a white bra and half-slip were chosen. Then after she steals the money and is changing for the ride to see Sam, we switched to a black bra and half-slip. Mr. Hitchcock wanted even the wardrobe to reflect the good and evil each of us has lurking within our inner selves.

I want to stop right here and set the record straight about an erroneous statement. It's not earth-shattering, but it bothered me because it indicated a lack of professionalism on my part. I may not be a lot of things, but I am professional. In an earlier book on Psycho, *Miss Colvig is quoted as saying, "Janet Leigh wanted her lingerie made to order. Mr. Hitchcock explained that it wouldn't work for the character, he wanted women to be able to identify with her wardrobe—maybe they even wore the same label. Janet had a lot of trouble with that."*

Now, that simply isn't so. As part of my research for this writing, I interviewed Rita Riggs, and she confirmed that I never asked for custom lingerie. Heck, never before in my life had any undies been made for me, so why would I have started then! I did wear one particular brand, however, because the cut fit me well. I had, and have, a small back and full breasts. Neither Rita nor I could remember the manufacturer's name, but she bought them over the counter—that's for sure!

Of course, the shower presented the most troublesome wardrobe challenge. How could nudity be implied without my actually being nude? I will address that obstacle a little later.

Makeup and hairstyle were relatively easy. Mr. Hitchcock and I both wanted the natural look. Only light street makeup was applied. My hair had been cut in Paris for *Perfect Furlough*, and I had kept it short during my pregnancy and, later, for the shooting of *Who Was That Lady?*

When I spoke to Joseph Stefano, as things were getting under way, he remarked upon how perfect my hair was for the film and thought I had styled it just for Marion. He didn't remember noticing my hair done that way before seeing me on the set.

It seems that Janet and Marion had already begun to meld.

FILMING

I wondered what it would be like on the set, working with a legend. I wasn't actually nervous, just excited. The first day the call sheet had Tony and me ready at 9:00 A.M. The scene was the exterior of the motel on the back lot, Marion driving up, the camera panning from the car to the front of the motel.

Hilton Green, first assistant director: "We always had the list of setups for the next day by the night before. That's why we were able to move so quickly, because Mr. Hitchcock was totally prepared. When he showed up that morning, we were all set to go, but he said, 'No, you don't start with your star in the very first shot. What else can we do?' Well, I went through about seventeen shots we could start with, and that's what he wanted to hear. I guess he was testing me to see if I knew every shot he had planned to do."

Hitch was true to his word. There were not extensive rehearsals, and what rehearsing we did was mostly for camera moves and actors' marks. If the scene played to his satisfaction— in other words, if we had dramatically fulfilled the goal of that particular shot—he didn't see the need for any more "takes." I will point out the few exceptions to that rule at the right time.

The atmosphere on the set was very calm and pleasant. The bulk of the creative process had already been done for Mr.

A good example of the camaraderie we shared on the set.

Hitchcock, so he was quite relaxed. Hitch and Tony and I liked to play games—word games, spelling games, Twenty Questions, anything like that. And I was the perfect foil for their kidding—I always have been an easy put-on. Then, there were the jokes, the risqué stories. We really did have enjoyable times between setups.

I can't forget to note how Hitch loved to scare me. I was never sure what would be in my dressing room when I came back from lunch. It seemed to me he was experimenting with Mother's appearance, using me as the guinea pig. Some hair-raising screams

emanated from behind my door when I walked in on these hideous, shriveled monstrosities sitting in my makeup chair.

Looking back now, I puzzle over whether this was just a gag or an effort to keep me a bit on edge, thus more in Marion's jittery state of mind.

Knowing Mr. Hitchcock, it could have been!

I did present Hitch with a surprise of my own, however. Because of the toilet's importance, I schemed with the prop man to put a regular potty in my dressing room, and then the still man took a picture of me sitting on the john reading the script. Hitch got a good chuckle from that.

There have been legions of words written about Mr. Hitchcock's treatment of his leading ladies. I can only relate my personal experience. He couldn't have been more considerate, or thoughtful, or respectful, or agreeable, or companionable. Even his detractors never doubted his genius as a filmmaker. I cannot think of a single complaint I could legitimately raise. Now, there may be some reasons why I had the experience I did. I was already established in my profession when I worked with him. I was not under contract to Mr. Hitchcock, so he was not in control of my career. I was married and we had socialized together with our spouses. Whatever any of that means!

To sum up, I tasted one of the most delicious adventures of my forty-nine years in Hollywood. I know that Anthony Perkins shared my feelings about Mr. Hitchcock, not only by my observations, but by statements from Berry Perkins (Tony's widow), Joseph Stefano, Hilton Green, and Peggy Robertson.

I think this is the time to tell a little more about Mr. Hitchcock's set demeanor. Curtis Harrington is a well-known film director who volunteered for this interview when he heard about the book. Mr. Harrington was under contract to Universal around 1969, and Mr. Hitchcock was shooting Topaz *on the lot at that time. He had always idolized Alfred Hitchcock; as he puts it, "Every young movie director in the business admires Hitchcock, to this day. His genius put him at the pinnacle of filmmaking." So Curtis asked the publicist on the picture, who was a friend, if there was a chance he could be a fly on the wall, an observer on the set of* Topaz. *Mr. Hitchcock had a "closed set," but the friend said he'd ask "the man." He returned with a welcome answer, "Mr. Hitchcock would be pleased—you're invited to come."*

Curtis Harrington: "I subsequently spent three entire days

watching him work. As I mentioned, I had expected to melt into the background, but Mr. Hitchcock took it upon himself to come to me between almost every take and explain what he was doing and why. I wasn't just an observer, he was teaching me. It turned out to be a really wonderful experience for me; he was so gracious, so kind. And I was able to ask him some interesting questions along the way.

"I was amazed because he would sit in his chair and tell the cameraman where to put the camera, but he would never look through the camera. Since I'm constantly checking to see my perimeters, I said, 'I'm surprised, Mr. Hitchcock, that you never look through the camera.' And he said, 'Well, why should I? I know what lens is on. I know where the camera is. So I know what I'm getting!'

"Can you imagine? That marvelous, complete confidence of years and years of filming!"

Curtis was privy to watching a pure Hitchcockian sequence being filmed for Topaz.

Curtis Harrington: "One of the heroines in the story was in an embrace with a man, and then she was shot by the man. It was so fascinating the way he filmed this; only Hitchcock, with his imaginative mind, would ever have thought of such a thing. He put the camera up in the rafters at the top of the set looking straight down on her. He showed her fall to the floor from the man's arms. She had on a long dress, and Hitchcock attached wires all the way around the base of the skirt. He practically had the whole crew on their bellies, and at a certain cue, they pulled each part of the skirt so it spread out as she fell, like a pool of blood, like a frame, like petals around the core of a flower. I believe he did it in slight slow motion, and it was just a marvelous moment."

Curtis then touched on a subject close to my heart—Mr. Hitchcock's directives to his actors.

Curtis Harrington: "In this one scene he was working with

fairly inexperienced performers, and I noticed Mr. Hitchcock gave the man and woman very, very specific physical instructions. I mean like, 'Now on that line you look down, you wait a beat, then you look back up at him, and hold.'

"*I didn't presume this was his ordinary method [I can vouch for that]. So I hesitantly ventured, 'It's fascinating to me that you are doing what you're doing, and I can see why you are doing it and what you are trying to achieve.' What I was fishing for was this—is that the way he always worked with actors, or not? And Mr. Hitchcock said, 'Well, Curtis, these are unseasoned players and I have to bring them a very long way in one picture.' I'll never forget; that was his exact quote.*"

As I, too, had discovered, Mr. Hitchcock could reach his objectives using all *directorial styles. He had no limitations.*

Curtis didn't escape becoming the barb of Hitchcock's wit, of course.

Curtis Harrington: "*Some years went by, and Mr. Hitchcock was in England making* Frenzy. *I happened to be in London during that period, and one night I was dining in one of those elegant restaurants that is also a private club. I saw Mr. Hitchcock at a nearby table with his wife and Joan Harrison [formerly a close associate]. I waited discreetly until they had finished their meal before going over to pay my respects. Mr. Hitchcock greeted me warmly and introduced me, and at that point his captain brought the check. He pulled out his wallet, and then looked up at me innocently. 'Oh, Curtis, I seem to have come out without any money.' I almost died; I didn't have that kind of money, on me or off me. But of course, it was just his delightful sense of humor.*"

Returning to the filming of *Psycho*, the day the opening scene was shot turned out to be quite a circus. The set was closed, which only made everyone outside all the more itchy to get a "look-see" inside.

What I was to wear was daring for the time. Appearing on screen clad only in undergarments was a taboo in 1959. I don't know why, but I really wasn't self-conscious. Maybe it was because there was actually less flesh exposed than there would have been if I were in a bathing suit or some décolleté evening gown. I rather enjoyed the fuss—being the first and all. But Mr. Hitchcock was very protective. Of course, he was also a showman, and the call for secrecy certainly didn't hurt the mystique of the project.

John Gavin was, and is, an extremely handsome man. And one of the nicest human beings on earth. His talents as a diplomat, obvious to us even then, were put to good use when he served as ambassador to Mexico for five years under two presidents. I have always liked him a great deal. To my knowledge, John has granted very few, if any, interviews regarding *Psycho*. I was extremely grateful he consented to talk to me. There were so many questions that had surfaced over the years, things John and I hadn't approached before. I was curious to know how he had reacted to Mr. Hitchcock's method of directing, which had unhinged so many other actors.

John Gavin: "I would like to say we all knew, or ultimately knew, we were working with a master, and I was thrilled to be in the picture. In answer to your inquiry, his way did not bother me at all. Quite the contrary. Because unlike you and the others, I was relatively new and only beginning to get the hang of it [acting], and in my estimation, up to then I was terrible. I was pretty bad. I understood a little bit about the technique of the camera, or at least the lenses and optics. So I liked the fact that Mr. Hitchcock said, 'At this point, we will have you in a full shot. And as you move here, it will be a waist shot. And then as you turn, come over here and say this, it will become a close-up.' I found that extremely helpful."

Strictly a publicity shot with me in my bad-girl bra.

It was always so difficult to have the first scene with a costar, someone you knew slightly but not really well, scheduled to be the steamy love scene. Not to mention the *beginning* of the movie. There we were, charting new waters with our wardrobe, or rather lack of it (John was bare-chested, while I was in my bra and half-slip).

It isn't easy to say, "Hello, nice to see you again," and then hop in the sack and make love. We were bound to be somewhat awkward.

I thought we had begun to warm up and were progressing fairly well. But Hitch kept asking for another take, which was very unlike him. Finally he called me over and quietly said, "I think you and John could be more passionate. See what you can do!"

He then had a word with John, before "rolling camera." I'm not sure exactly what we did differently (I know I did attempt to be more intimate—within reason, of course), but whatever it was clicked, and we had the print.

All this time, I've wondered what he said to John. Did Hitch also ask him to see what he could do?

John Gavin: "I think I would have recollected that. No."

So now I know—I was the one Hitch had "used." By this time, I'm sure you understand how much I adored Hitch. But he did have that mischievous mind. And I wouldn't have put it past him to pull my chain, and then to pull John's chain—just to get the desired results.

He wanted to show the real compulsion for my later actions, and knowing I shared his brand of humor, he figured he would let me do the spurring on—so to speak.

In my early conversations with Joseph Stefano, he mentioned he had always felt that Marion loved Sam more than Sam loved her. Joe didn't believe Sam couldn't have found a way to marry Marion if he had really wanted to—he never believed he was that weak. I remember adding, "As it stood, Sam had no problem and no commitment."

By making Marion a bit more ardent than Sam, was Hitch telling the audience that she loved him more? Thus making her death even more tragic, more pathetic.

John Gavin: "They say the devil knows more because he's old than because he's the devil. And I wish I could go back and do a lot of things again with my current understanding and knowledge. One of my sense memories—Mr. Hitchcock sat close to us during that scene, right near the camera. And for a while there, for a long while, I was having a very difficult time. Because somebody had a terrible B.O. problem. . . ."

Janet: "My God, I hope it wasn't me!"

John Gavin: "No, no! I finally figured out it was Mr. Hitchcock's cigar. Or more correctly, the breath from the actual cigar. It was very distracting."

I was absolutely hysterical. I didn't have an inkling anything like that had happened. Maybe this insight will help the reader to understand some of the human hurdles performers have to overcome.

I told John about my first screen kiss on my first picture, Romance of Rosy Ridge. *I was so nervous I made Van Johnson, a real pro, tense also. The director, Roy Rowland, finally solved my dilemma. He said, "It's not Janet kissing Van, it's Lissy Anne [my character] kissing Henry [Van's character]."*

But it is strange to pucker up with fifty or so onlookers.

John Gavin: "Maybe it was the time, but I consider most films, and specifically Hitchcock films, to have had a good deal of suggestion of fireworks [in an emotional moment] if you will. As a matter of fact, he used fireworks in To Catch a Thief when Grace Kelly's and Cary Grant's lips met, as the Bastille Day celebration of fireworks illuminated the sky. All of those implications have a level of taste."

Janet: "We were under the strictures of censorship, so we couldn't show anything explicit going on between us, John. Absolutely nothing. But the imagination was given free rein to *participate. It was so sensual; our scene was so sensual."*

John Gavin: "Dear Janet, please don't go on. You're getting me excited!

"It's true. The audience has been robbed of their inventiveness. Today they would just show the two actually copulating."

All the filming I was involved in was done at the studio except for the used car lot where Marion traded in her car. The car lot is still there, but now it is a BMW dealership. It's much more efficient working under controlled circumstances that allow for more intense concentration. Hitch preferred it this way as well.

John told of an interesting set incident, one that showed a slightly more flexible Mr. Hitchcock.

John Gavin: "When the final scene with Tony was completed, Tony asked, 'Do you mind if we do another take where we do it a little differently?' I'm paraphrasing Tony to Mr. Hitchcock now: "You have it this way. What would you think if I turned to the left instead of the right—or whatever the issue was—and then you can choose which version you like best.' And Mr. Hitchcock agreed."

Janet: "I'll bet my bottom dollar Tony's change did not affect the camera position!"

John Gavin: "You're absolutely right. Nor did it alter my movement, because I had to go after him wherever he went."

In digging for information at the Academy library, I began to feel like an archaeologist searching for long-lost artifacts—except the passage of thirty-five years doesn't quite put us into that category. It was there that I came across an interview with Anthony Perkins, in which he told about another scene where he had made suggestions to Hitchcock. It was a lengthy exchange between Norman and detective Arbogast, and Tony—timidly in the beginning—brought up his concept of the scene, which included some dialogue changes.

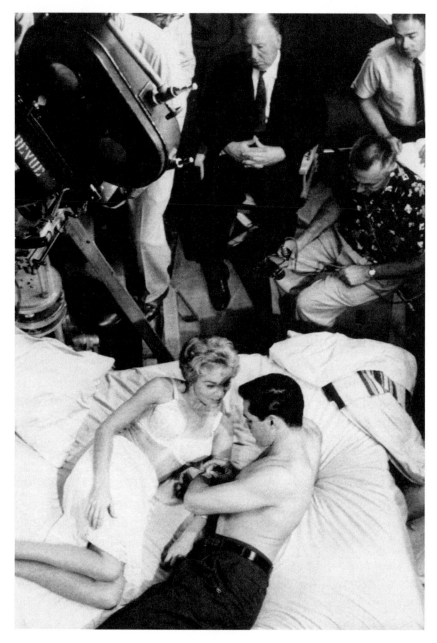

Is Janet pulling John's chain?

Tony was a little put out because Hitchcock didn't seem thrilled to be distracted from his London Times. *Then Hitchcock lowered the paper and said, "Oh, they're [the changes] all right—I'm sure they're all right. Have you given these a lot of thought? You've really thought it out? And you like these changes?" Tony assured Hitchcock that he did indeed. And the director said simply, "All right, that's the way we'll do it."*

I'll say it again: I betcha Tony's ideas did not *involve a camera move.*

Still, just when you think you might have Alfred Hitchcock figured out, he surprises you yet again.

It's odd how a word can keep tripping you up. In the real estate office, when Cassidy, the rude oilman (played to the hilt by Frank Albertson), talked about buying off unhappiness, he asked Marion if she was unhappy. Marion replied, "Not inordinately."

Well, that became a tongue twister, and I stumbled over it a few times. I've heard other performers express similar problems; it seems that on every film there is always some phrase or word that causes trouble. I guess we should be grateful if we have only one faux pas a picture. Hitch must have experienced this sort of thing before, because the retakes didn't faze him in the least. It invariably provoked me, however. I don't like to make dumb mistakes. (Who does?)

The driving sequence was done on a stage using process plates, or special effects. Process shooting means that footage, already shot on location, is projected onto a large screen at the rear, while another camera photographs the actors playing a scene in the foreground. Technically it is difficult (or so they tell me), since the film frames on each camera have to be synchronized. I know it is a laborious operation, because the rear projection has to be rewound to the same spot after each take. Fortunately, as I've mentioned, Hitch was usually a director of few takes.

Except for the opening with John Gavin, the scene at the real estate office, and the parlor scene with Tony Perkins, I was pretty much doing a pantomime in this highly charged film. Obviously this is quite demanding, as you have no one to play off or respond to, no give-and-take. It's just you. Hitch was invaluable in the car progressions. He knew the dialogue of the voices he planned to superimpose, so he read the various characters' parts aloud to me—Sam; the car salesman and the officer; the boss and the secretary; the boss and Lila; the boss and Cassidy. That way I could let my face reflect my thoughts as I imagined these conversations. It was tricky, but we did it.

Joseph Stefano: "At a film festival recently, someone said, 'In all of your writing, you always seem to want to put a person alone against whatever the situation is. Even in Psycho, *Marion Crane was alone. Why is that?'*

"I think what most attracts me is the human condition that ultimately, basically, we are all alone. And that the only thing that makes fire is when somebody else who is alone collides with us in an emotional way, and then we have love. So my feeling was this story in regard to Marion was all about her love; everything she did, even to being killed, was about her love. And that made her a lone character."

When I was alone in front of the camera without the illusory voices, I composed a running conversation in my mind, so that the audience could sense what Marion was thinking about. In the packing scene, Marion might have had these fleeting thoughts: What was her sister going to say? Would Lila hate her or forgive her? Would Sam go along with her rash behavior? Should she take more things? The pang of guilt when she walked by the picture of her mother and father on her dresser!—I'm sure you get the idea.

For every day I have ever worked on a film, I have thanked my Lord for Lillian Burns Sidney. From the first time I read a scene with her at MGM to the present day (I'm still trying to get it right), she guided and led me toward an understanding of this profession and my craft. She helped me to recognize holes and weak spots in a script. She showed me how to create the reality of a role, how to make the character mine.

It was she who taught me how to approach a part. Take Marion, for example. I invented a complete life for Marion Crane. I knew where she went to school, what church she attended, what kind of a student, daughter, friend, and relative she was. I knew her likes, dislikes, color preferences, favorite foods, favorite book, favorite movie. I knew her secrets, her passions, her fantasies, her fears. I knew her intimately.

So when Marion appeared in the first shot, the audience was meeting a complete person, a unique person, as each of us is unique.

When I met with Joseph Stefano, I asked him what he was most proud of in terms of his contribution to the film and its success.

Joseph Stefano: "I think the screenplay I wrote was just about exactly right. I found the level for me of the movie. After all, I was a young Italian-American man, born in south Philadelphia, went into show business as a singer and dancer, then began to write, wrote a script that sold for a Sophia Loren movie, and suddenly I'm sitting in a room with Alfred Hitchcock. And I know nothing about motels, that kind of life. I'd never even been to Arizona. So it was kind of like I had to find where to set this movie in my own consciousness, in my own experience, and I think that what I did was to create a universe for it. So I could tell you what was going on in other houses nearby, the people who had been at the motel yesterday who didn't get killed. I knew all that. It's the way I devised the universe in which I placed these people that actors were going to portray on the screen. I felt that the extraordinary thing about Psycho was that I had hit almost a visual nerve."

Joe had defined the process: creating a universe.

Working with Anthony Perkins was the ultimate adventure. He was so exciting, such an inspired actor. Even before shooting began, he had come up with a delicious bit of quirky business which absolutely delighted Hitchcock. Tony thought Norman should munch on bits of candy corn throughout the film. It was extremely effective, right on target. Just like the inventor himself.

It was a treat every time we tackled a new scene. I was always anxious to see what course Norman would choose this time. And no matter how well I knew what I was going to bring to the scene, his presentation would automatically trigger a different and fuller response from Marion.

There was this constant reaching for more, more, which made the moments richer and more fulfilling. The set was alive, sparkling with electricity and energy. Yet it was all inside; you could feel it waiting to escape and explode. But the exterior appeared calm, unruffled, even effortless. Being a part of this was a privilege I will treasure forever.

Berry Berenson Perkins, Anthony Perkins's wife: "Tony and I worked together in a Bob Altman production, Remember My Name. *He couldn't believe I would go out on the set and not even think about it (the scene) and just do it. I believe he spent a lot of time working on the inner self, delving into the intent of the film, and then projecting it onto the screen."*

John Gavin: "I don't know how Tony was with you [Janet], but I do believe he was this way with everybody. He was a dedicated, generous actor, but when the scene was over, he would go to his dressing room. I didn't take that as rudeness, or aloofness, I took that as wanting to think about the work, and I respected that. He was always very nice, but contacts were almost entirely on the set. Then something happened which endeared him to me forever. One day he came up to me and told me how good he thought I was. I was pretty self-conscious then, so for him to say, 'You're really good, better than I thought,' meant a great deal."

I would presume that in his preparation for a role, Tony dug very deep indeed. And took the time to formulate his interpretation. Because Anthony Perkins was a real pro.

THE
SHOWER

T he bathroom scenes were scheduled to be shot December 17 through December 23, 1959. It's ironic when you think of it: During the day I was in the throes of being stabbed to death, and at night I was wrapping presents from Santa Claus for the children. And hubby. And family. And friends. Christmas was always a big celebration for me; the spirit of the holiday itself meant so much. When I was a young girl in Stockton, California, and we didn't have very much, it was a festive occasion nonetheless. The choirs I belonged to in church and school would go all over the city singing Christmas carols for different groups and clubs. We usually traveled to Merced, California, to visit Grandma and Grandpa Morrison. And I still joyfully anticipated whatever little gifts we could scrape together. So finally, when I was earning a good living, I was able to really make a point of going all out for everybody.

Evening was the time for me to be the wife as well as the mother, the two identities that have always had priority over everything else in my life. As I worked on *Psycho*, my husband, Tony Curtis, was making *Rat Race* with our friend Debbie Reynolds. So, between the two of us, there was always a great deal to discuss at dinner. Aside from comparing notes about our respective films, we were concerned about Debbie, who had been through a difficult time the year before with her divorce from Eddie Fisher. The public only sees the actor's screen persona and rarely understands what a toll personal tragedies can take on a creative individual.

Fortunately, Mr. Hitchcock did not like to work late. Some directors never seemed to want to go home and kept slave hours. But not Hitch!

Hilton Green: "Our crew, coming from television, was used to a shorter shooting schedule, doing more setups in a day. Mr. Hitchcock never wanted to work past six P.M. And he had one standing engagement: Every Thursday, Mr. Hitchcock and madame would have a quiet dinner at Chasen's. So on Thursdays we finished even earlier than usual."

As Christmas approached, the question consuming me during the day was: what to wear in the shower? Rita Riggs and I pored over magazines that showed wardrobe suggestions for strippers. Every guy on the set was eager to look and give his opinion on what would work. The pictures were entertaining—we all laughed for hours—but hardly practical. There was an impressive display of pinwheels, feathers, sequins, toy propellers, balloons, etc., but nothing suitable for our needs. Rita solved the puzzle. Nude-colored moleskin! Over the vital parts! Perfect!

Neither of us ever thought about negative consequences. But there were a few. Water had the tendency to melt the adhesive, for one. Plus wearing the moleskin for any length of time made my skin raw when we peeled it off. So we would remove it between shots to give my skin some relief, which, of course, was time-consuming.

Before the actual filming began, Mr. Hitchcock showed me the storyboards, drawn for the shower montage by the brilliant artist Saul Bass, who also did the titles for the movie. There were anywhere from seventy-one to seventy-eight angles planned for the series, each one lasting for two to three seconds on the screen. But whether an image appeared on screen for two seconds or two minutes or twenty minutes, it took just as long to prepare for a camera setup; the groundwork was the same.

Years later, at the American Film Institute tribute to Mr. Hitchcock, Tony and I presented one segment. In the dialogue prepared by George Stevens, Jr., who is meticulous in his research, it is said there were seventy-one setups; however, in another book on Psycho, *it was stated there were seventy-eight. In all the interviews Chris and I conducted for this book and in all the searching we did at Universal, Paramount, and the Academy, we found no verification of the exact number. Therefore the number remains vague to this day.*

The shower sequence was the exception to Hitchcock's attitude toward film editing. This next series of shots *depended* on the cutting to startle and terrify, which is why he was so careful about following the storyboard. The word "cutting" is appropriate here, because the quick flashes were meant to be indicative of the continuous slashing, plunging knife.

Now is an appropriate time to address another popular question:

Did Saul Bass direct the shower scene, as he claims?

This is an easy one—a definite "absolutely not!" I have emphatically said this in any interview I've ever given. I've said it to his face in front of other people. For the life of me, I cannot understand what possessed Saul Bass to make that statement. He is a celebrated designer of titles, a three-time Academy Award nominee as a producer of animated short films, and so forth and so on. Why would he say that? Why would he need to do that? Mr. Hitchcock and everyone else associated with Psycho *acknowl-*

edged Mr. Bass for his contributions. The movie credits read:
Titles Designed by Saul Bass, Pictorial Consultant—Saul Bass.

I was in that shower for seven days, and, believe you me,
Alfred Hitchcock was right next to his camera for every one of
those seventy-odd shots.

Lillian Burns Sidney gave me some prudent advice after the
successful release of my first film. The studio was buzzing about

*its newest star. "One film does not a star make," she told me.
"Come back in twenty years, then maybe you'll be a star." I
never forgot it. Now I have some advice for Mr. Bass: "Drawing
some pictures does not a director make."*

*I am not the only one who has been incensed by Bass's asser-
tion. Joseph Stefano and Rita Riggs have voiced their dismay at
Mr. Bass's claims as well. And listen to Hilton.*

*Hilton Green: "Saul might have visited the set, but I don't
recall him there that much, maybe a half day in all. There is not
a shot in that movie that I didn't roll the camera for. And I can
tell you I never rolled the camera for Mr. Bass.*

*"I have been quoted before, and you can quote me again,
because I am very outspoken on this matter."*

I hope this puts that rumor to bed once and for all.

For Marion, going into the shower was more than just a
need to wash away the day's grime. Hitch and I discussed the

implications at great length. Marion had decided to go back to Phoenix, come clean, and take the consequences, so when she stepped into the tub it was as if she were stepping into the baptismal waters. The spray beating down on her was purifying the corruption from her mind, purging the evil from her soul. She was like a virgin again, tranquil, at peace.

If I could convey this to the audience, the attack would become even more horrifying and appalling.

The seven days in the water were trying for everyone. There

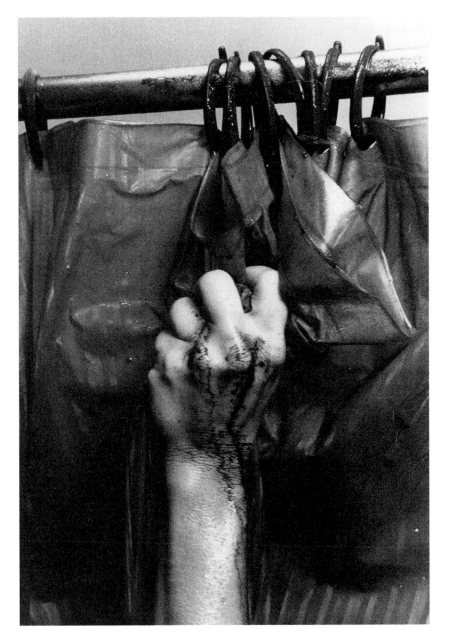

were many repeats of the same action, taken from different angles. Then there were the delays due to moleskin problems or camera technicalities. We were fortunate that the cast and crew were patient and had a sense of humor, because these circumstances could have caused some flare-ups.

By the way, contrary to what is said on the Psycho *tour at Universal Studios, Mr. Hitchcock did not turn on the cold water to get a shocked reaction from me when Mother came in. I was able to do that all by myself, thank you very much. In fact, he was adamant about the water temperature being very comfortable.*

Security was a constant source of trouble. Even though I wore the moleskin, I was still pretty much . . . on display, so to speak. I didn't want strangers lurking around, hoping to get a peek in case of any accidental mishap. If anything did slip up, at least only my friends would get a look.

Hitch didn't want extra people around either—for my sake, of course, but also I'm sure to keep the hype going about what was *really* happening on that crazy set!

When I was in the tub looking up toward the showerhead, I was surprised at how many gaffers (electricians) were on the overhead scaffolding. I hadn't seen that many technicians up there even during elaborate scenes on the huge stages, let alone for one person in a tiny bathroom. And each one must have had two or three "assistants." I have a hunch they worked dirt cheap on those days.

One of the toughest shots in the entire film—for me anyway—was at the end of the murder scene. The camera started on a close-up of the dead eye, then gradually pulled back to include more and more of the tub, the shower, the bathroom, until it was very high (as from a bird's-eye view? A *stuffed* bird's-eye view?).

As I mentioned earlier, I could not wear the special contact lenses the scene seemed to require and "going it alone" was not easy. I would blink involuntarily, or swallow, or breathe. On my slide down the tiled wall and collapse over the edge, I had landed in the most awkward position—my mouth and nose were squished against the side of the tub. And drops from the splashing water settled upon my eyelashes and brows and face, and they tickled. It was a formidable task not to react.

The camera didn't have the automatic focus in 1959, so the operator had to do it manually, changing it as the camera moved. Very demanding. So—again the exception to the Hitchcock rule—there were many takes on this shot. Somewhere in the twenties—Hilton Green and I both agreed between twenty-two and twenty-six. Everyone was keeping their fingers crossed. We were almost near the end and nothing had gone wrong. Hallelujah!

At that moment (thanks to Hitch's compassionate insistence on warm water), I could feel the damn moleskin pulling away from my left breast. I knew the lens would not pick it up—that part was below the top of the tub. But I also knew the guys in the balcony would get an eyeful. By that time, I was sore where I was pressed against the ungiving porcelain—my body ached—and I didn't want to shoot this again if we didn't have to. So I decided not to say anything—the hell with it, I said to myself; let 'em look!

Time to deal with another question:

Did Hitchcock try to persuade you to be nude in the shower?

Mr. Hitchcock never asked me to do the scene nude. I would like to explain something at this point. This book was intended to set the record straight about Psycho *by sharing unknown stories, incidents, and memories. So when we reread most of what has been written and said about* Psycho, *and spoke with so many of the actual participants, we felt even more compelled to correct the blatant inaccuracies and lingering tall tales.*

There would have been no point in Hitch suggesting that I

play the scene nude, because the industry operated under the scrutiny of a censor's office. Every script and finished product had to be approved by this board. And nudity was not allowed to be shown. And you know what else? Doing the scene nude would have cheated Hitch and millions of movie fans, because all would have missed his mastery of insinuating situations and conditions.

If you had looked at the storyboard, you would have noticed that there was no need to see the whole body nude: One angle would show an arm here, a tummy there, shoulders down to the great divide, legs, back.

(The back—one of the sexiest parts of the body. For a scene in The Vikings, Kirk Douglas ripped my gown down the back, exposing the whole length of skin to the lowest hollow. He has always believed the back is a real turn-on.)

Joseph Stefano cleared up a couple of other points. Mr. Hitchcock did not say to him, "I'm going to have a problem with Janet; she thinks her breasts are too big!" (I would have had to be pretty stupid to worry about my boobs being too big. Actually I often say, "Thank you, God.")

Stefano also told me about another erroneously printed statement: "I never said anything to anyone about a trembling actress." (This refers to a remark Hitchcock allegedly made to Stefano about the possibility of me appearing nude in the shower: "I don't want to deal with a trembling actress.")

Another question:

Were you really in the shower?

I am amazed that I am still asked that question. You look at that sequence closely and you see—me! Unquestionably, without a doubt, unequivocally, I was in that shower for seven drenching days. I was in that shower so much that my skin was beginning to look like a wrinkled prune.

Every player has a stand-in. And on most dangerous stunts,

the movie's insurance coverage insists on stunt doubles as well. Although sometimes we fudge a bit and do more of the stunts than we really should—it can be fun! (Of course, you have to be a mite zany to think that way. But we all have some of that daredevil craziness in us.)

On Psycho, *Mr. Hitchcock hired a body double, a professional artists' model who was accustomed to being nude, it being all in a day's work. Her name was Marli Renfro, and she was paid $400 a week, one week guaranteed. He used Ms. Renfro to see how much of the body outline the camera would pick up behind the shower curtain, and to test the density of the water—what level of water force would read well and yet not obscure Marion. But she was not on camera during the shower scene.*

At the end of the murder, Norman wrapped the corpse in the shower curtain and dragged it out to the car. That was the only shot I was not in. Hitch showed me that no one could see who it was, so there was no need for me to be bounced around. I totally agreed.

However, my naughty friend Mr. Hitchcock did try to slip one shot by the inspectors.

Joseph Stefano: "He [Hitchcock] knew he would never get away with frontal nudity, but he thought he might squeak by with a high overhead shot of Marion lying over the tub. For this shot he used the model. But her buttocks were seen. The incredible thing was that the scene right before this one was when he went to your [Janet's] eye and it was heartbreaking. There was no sex connected to it at all. There was this beautiful person whom I had cared about all through the movie up to this point, and she was lying there dead. But no deal. It was the only angle from the shower sequence that was cut."

The day they were filming that long shot, John Gavin had quite an awakening.

John Gavin: "I had rooms at the studio [Universal]; I used one as an office. I noticed on the call sheet that the shower montage was still being shot, so I came by to say hello. [He didn't realize I, Janet, was finished with my part.] The sign read Closed Set, and I thought, 'Well, it's not closed to me, I belong to this company.' So I opened the door and went in. And indeed, no one said a boo. I walked around and all of a sudden I noticed this girl just wandering about absolutely stark naked. My eyes almost fell out of my head, like a great lout. But no one else was paying any attention to her; I guess they had become quite used to her."

Every person we spoke with who had been involved with the movie was dumbfounded that anyone could think it wasn't me in the shower. But once people got wind that there was a nude model on the set at all, it was fireworks for trivia.

You know what I think? I think Hitch deliberately hired the model partly to plant the seed in people's minds that this picture had nudity. He had started to manipulate the audiences before the film was even in a theater. He teased the pros, the nonpros, the sophisticated, and the naive. He knew the rumor would eventually become the gospel truth. The seed would blossom to such an extent that when the viewers came out of the movie houses, they would swear on the Bible that they had seen nudity. And gushing blood. And weapon penetration. Such was Alfred Hitchcock's gift.

INTERMISSION

A prime example of how artfully Hitchcock blended location footage and studio-shot close-ups in *Psycho* is the tense exchange between an obviously nervous Marion (on the road with $40,000 in stolen money) and a leery highway patrolman played by actor Mort Mills. Janet wasn't required for the film shot on Highway 99, as Marion is not visible to the audience when the scene opens with the cop approaching Marion's car, which is parked on the shoulder of the road and looks to be unoccupied.

The scene switches to studio-shot film with the first glimpse of Marion from the officer's point of view: She is sleeping across the front seat of her car and sits up, startled, when the cop taps on the window. The scene progresses with a series of back-and-forth head shots between Janet and Mills as Marion is questioned. When Marion is allowed to drive away, Hitchcock places Janet at a prop dashboard in front of a rear-projected film of Mills, from the location shoot, climbing into his patrol car to follow Marion. Audiences watching this scene play out would swear that Janet had actually been out on Highway 99 with Mills, so cleverly is the film lit, shot, and edited.

From a theatrical standpoint, this nerve-wracking interruption in Marion's journey is classic Hitchcock as it incorporates several of the director's favorite themes.

The screen-filling close-up of the cop wearing mirrored sun-

glasses and a passive, yet intimidating, expression as he stares at Marion through her car window, is, in the opinion of Janet's daughter, Jamie Lee Curtis, "the scariest moment in the film." And it reflects Hitchcock's own well-known terror of police. Although based in car-obsessed Los Angeles for most of his life, Hitch never learned how to drive, apparently because of a very real fear that if he did, he might be pulled over for a traffic infraction.

The scene's suspense derives from a typical Hitchcock setup:

Marion and the audience know that she is harboring thousands of dollars in stolen money in her purse, but the patrolman, of course, does not. Will he discover Marion's secret loot? Hitch adroitly handles this tension by having Marion carefully turn her back to the officer (but *toward* the audience) and remove the envelope of stolen money from her purse as she feigns a search for her driver's license. There is a touch of Hitchcockian irony as well in a remark the cop makes after realizing Marion has spent the night in her car. "You should have stayed in a motel," he admonishes her, "just to be safe." And finally, the director's penchant for scatological humor surfaces in a close-up of Marion's license plate: ANL-709.

The only scene in which Janet *was* filmed on location (at a used car lot located just a few miles north of Universal Studios) also required an undetectable studio-shot insert. After agreeing to pay $700 to trade in her car for one with California plates, Marion retreats to the rest room, where she counts out the money from her envelope of stolen cash.

Although the actual car lot housed a rest room, there was no way to wedge a film crew into it, so the scene was shot at the studio on a set that cost only $200 to construct. Again, Hitch's precise techniques make it impossible to distinguish between the footage of Janet shot on location and that which she filmed back at Revue.

With Janet's scenes completed at the end of December, Hitchcock concentrated on getting all of Anthony Perkins's performance on film, as the actor was needed in Manhattan to begin rehearsals for the Frank Loesser musical *Greenwillow,* scheduled for a March 8 opening at the Alvin Theater.

One of the most interesting challenges Hitch faced in regard to Perkins's performance had little to do with the actor himself. The director felt it was essential, for the sake of *Psycho*'s surprise ending, that audiences not be able to recognize Tony's voice when Norman is speaking as Mother. So rather than try to dis-

guise Perkins's delivery of the dialogue, Hitchcock hired three actors to create the harsh, scolding tones of the deceased matriarch of the Bates family.

Perkins's good friend Paul Jasmin had developed a comic vocal portrait of a crotchety old woman whom he dubbed Eunice Harris. For laughs—and with the encouragement of pals Elaine Stritch and Stanley Kubrick—Jasmin would affect Eunice's "no-bullshit, Marjorie Main–type voice" and place late-night prank phone calls to the likes of Rosalind Russell.

After listening to a tape of Jasmin as Eunice, Hitchcock agreed that the cranky-voiced lady had a distinctive sound, and Jasmin was hired to record Mrs. Bates's dialogue. "He sent me to a dubbing room," Jasmin remembers, "and I just did it scene by scene for an assistant while Hitchcock was on the set shooting. . . . I had to do it again and again. The woman's voice was really shrewish. That's the quality Hitchcock liked."

Hitch also relied on the voices of veteran character actresses Virginia Gregg and Jeanette Nolan to add to Mother's distinctive sound. Nolan, married to actor John McIntire, who was playing Sheriff Chambers in the film, recalls, "I had next to no contact with Mr. Hitchcock. I simply went to the recording studio and looped [dubbed] some of Mother's lines. I also recall doing quite a lot of screaming for the film."

(Some of Nolan's screams were mixed with those of Vera Miles for *Psycho*'s climax, when Lila discovers Mrs. Bates corpse in the fruit cellar. Nolan's screams were *not* used to enhance the shower murder. "Those were all my screams," Janet says, "although we did have to overdub some of them later so that they could be heard over the sound of the running water.")

Hitchcock's technical mastery in blending the disparate vocal performances of his three actors surprised Paul Jasmin, who was unable, at first, to identify his contributions in the finished film. "Hitchcock was more brilliant than I thought," he recalls. "In postproduction, he spliced and blended a mixture of [the three

voices] so that who's speaking literally changes from word to word and sentence to sentence. He did that to confuse the audience. I recognize my voice before Tony carries Mother down the stairs. But the very last speech, the monologue, is all done by a woman—Virginia, with probably a little of Jeanette spliced in."

This last speech of Mother's (heard by the audience as Norman's thoughts while he sits in his jail cell) is markedly different in tone from the character's earlier ravings. And appropriately so. According to the psychiatrist's explanation, Norman has now completely *become* Mother, and his/her voice reflects that. There is no need now for scolding or humiliating. The voice is softer, more feminine, almost seductive; clearly that of a woman, as opposed to that of a woman being impersonated by a man.

Production memos indicate that Hitch *did* technically alter Tony Perkins's voice on the *Psycho* sound track for one line of dialogue. Immediately following the shower murder, the camera pulls back from Marion's lifeless eye to pan her motel room, pausing for a moment on the folded newspaper that contains the stolen money, and finally passes through the window to rest on the Bates house, silhouetted against a dark sky of shifting clouds. From the house we hear Norman shout, "Mother! Oh God, Mother. Blood. . . Blood!" Hitchcock directed his sound technicians to remove the bass line from Tony's voice for this moment, resulting in Norman sounding weirdly adolescent.

The second murder in *Psycho,* that of private investigator Arbogast, played by Martin Balsam, proved to be just as tricky a technical proposition as Marion's demise in the shower had been. Arbogast, snooping around the Bates property, enters the house quietly with the intention of questioning Mother about Marion's disappearance. After a cursory look around the foyer, Arbogast decides to climb the stairs to the second floor, where he believes Mrs. Bates is sequestered.

As he proceeds up the stairs, the camera climbs above him so that at the moment he reaches the second-floor landing, the audience point of view is from the ceiling directly above his head. Suddenly, Mother races out of a side door and stabs Arbogast in the forehead with a knife. In shock from the blow, Arbogast loses his footing and falls backward down the stairs, his arms flailing the air helplessly. He lands on his back on the oriental rug at the

foot of the stairs, and instantly Mother swoops upon him again, thrusting the knife deep into his chest.

Hitchcock chose the overhead camera angle in an effort to obscure the fact that Mother was Norman in drag. (For the same reason, he used a similar setup for a later scene in which Norman carries his mother's corpse to the fruit cellar.)

The brief, spine-tingling scene of Arbogast's murder—an unexpected, startling follow-up to the shower murder—entailed rigging a movable camera track run on pulleys that could glide alongside the staircase in tandem with Arbogast's fall. As with the close-up of Marion's dead eye, the camera operator was forced to move the camera and focus the lens simultaneously, an arduous task in the days prior to computerized camera handling.

In addition, a chairlike contraption had to be constructed on the stairs in which Martin Balsam could sit, lean back, and wave his arms around simulating Arbogast's terrifying backward fall as the mechanism moved him down the staircase in complete safety.

"That scene took weeks of preparation," recalls Hilton Green. "We would rehearse it, with a stand-in for Marty, every chance we got after completing other scenes on the picture. [For the overhead shots] we had to build a platform suspended from the ceiling that could accommodate a camera operator and the then-heavy camera equipment. And for all of our precautions, I think Marty Balsam did suffer some minor back problems from the shot."

The interior of the Bates house had been constructed on the old Universal stage where the 1925 Lon Chaney horror classic *The Phantom of the Opera* had been filmed. "I'm almost positive," says Green, laughing, "that if you were to go over to the *Phantom* stage and look up into the rafters, you'd find that *Psycho* platform still hanging there today."

For years, there has been misinformation perpetuated about the Arbogast murder footage. Because Hitchcock was bedridden with the flu on January 14, the day the scene was scheduled to be shot, it's been stated that Hilton Green (aided by Hitchcock from his sickbed phone) directed the complicated scene.

"I didn't direct the entire scene," Green says emphatically. "Absolutely not." With Hitchcock's explicit storyboards—which illustrated every detail of the action to be filmed—Green shot "just Martin Balsam coming in the front door, looking around, and starting up the stairs prior to Mother's entrance." Hitchcock's assistant, Peggy Robertson, remembers showing Green's footage to her boss when he returned to the studio: "We were all very proud of ourselves, and when they finished running the film, Hitch said, 'Well, that's fine. A very good job. Of course, we can't use it.' And we all looked at each other and said, 'What do you mean?'

"'You've got the thing reversed,'" Hitchcock replied. "'What we want to see is a man in peril going upstairs, where we think death might await him. What you've shot [looks like] a murderer going upstairs, about to kill someone.'"

"We didn't really know what he was talking about," Robertson admits. "And then he said, 'Well, let's look at what you shot. You've got a close-up of Arbogast's hand on a banister, a close-up of his feet going up the stairs, all very threatening. You need it the other way around.' So we redid the scene shot from the top of the staircase, showing Martin Balsam coming up the stairs in trepidation." (A few of the Hilton Green shots of Balsam's feet and hands did make it into the final print of the picture.)

Filming of the scenes involving John Gavin and Vera Miles progressed without incident. Miles's most famous scene in the film, when her character, Lila, encounters Mother's petrified remains, proved to be another technical challenge, and an unexpected one.

"Hitch was very upset about that," Green remembers. "After Lila comes down the cellar stairs, she touches Mother on the shoulder and the corpse swings around in her chair. Lila screams and her hand shoots up involuntarily, knocking a hanging bare lightbulb, causing it to swing and cast those eerie shadows on Mother's shriveled skull. Hitch wanted a flare of light in the camera at the same time the corpse swung around. First of all, it was very difficult to get Mother to turn—a prop man had to be squatting down on the back of his heels, out of sight, turning the chair in unison with the hitting of the lightbulb, in sync with the movement of the camera. Trying to get all of that in one precise moment proved extremely tough. Oh, I've never seen Hitch so furious. He looked at the dailies and it wasn't the way he wanted.

"He got mad at me, and hollered, 'You didn't get that shot right. You didn't get the flare.' Well, the cameraman, Jack Russell, was standing right there, and Hitch's comments were obviously meant for him too, but it was done indirectly. This was the way Mr. Hitchcock operated. Everybody got the message, and we had to go back and shoot the scene a second time, just to get the flare right."

Filming on *Psycho* wrapped on February 1, 1960. With Janet having been off the picture for a month and Anthony Perkins busy with pre-Broadway performances of *Greenwillow*, Hitch dispensed with the traditional wrap party. After less than a week's rest, he plunged into postproduction chores on the picture, which would include designing a publicity campaign and screening policy for *Psycho* that would, at first, dismay distributors and theater managers, alienate movie critics—and titillate moviegoers.

C.N.

JUNE 1960: THE RELEASE

Six months into the year, Princess Margaret had married the commoner Anthony Armstrong-Jones; the laser beam had successfully been used for eye surgery; and Khrushchev was still denouncing U.S. policies at the United Nations.

We sang songs such as "Camelot" and "What's the Matter With Kids Today?" We took pleasure in stage musicals like *Bye Bye Birdie* and *The Unsinkable Molly Brown,* and devoured the bestsellers *To Kill a Mockingbird* and *Born Free.*

Jackie Kennedy was pregnant with John-John and Patricia Kennedy Lawford asked me to host a kickoff luncheon in September for Senator John Fitzgerald Kennedy's presidential campaign.

And the movie *Psycho* was released.

Before I tell you all about the film's opening, I want to share with you my reactions the first time I saw *Psycho*. It was in a screening room at Universal Studios. I honestly don't remember who was there besides the Hitchcocks and the Wassermans, but I recall the room was full. I was very nervous. Throughout my career, whenever I saw myself on the screen, I was never completely satisfied. I knew the extent of the emotion that I had put into a scene, and somehow, when it was projected, I usually felt a portion of the passion had been lost. And I did so want to be good, to do justice to Mr. Hitchcock. And to Marion.

At the conclusion of the film, I was stupefied and electrified at the same time. I had fallen right into Hitch's trap; this supposedly enlightened fly had flown blindly into the master's web. I believed I was watching a tale unfold that was to be about Marion—her great love, her temptation, her empathy for Norman's pain, her resolution. And then she was gone, brutally gone—and I realized I had taken the wrong story turn, just as Marion had gone off the main highway, just as Mr. Hitchcock had orchestrated. I couldn't get over how I had been baited. And I had read the book and the script. I was there, Charlie.

When we were shooting the shower montage, because of the repetitions and the fact that we'd done the scene in bits and pieces, I was not totally scared. Don't get me wrong—when Mother threw open the curtains, I was damn frightened. But obviously I was not constantly in a state of hysteria or I would have ended up in a loony bin myself.

When I saw it edited and scored, however, I had the perpetual screaming meemies. I felt every thrust of that knife, screamed with every lunge. I was completely terrorized.

Then the picture started on the real path, Norman's plight, and I was going shakily along with it, when whammo, I was hit with another staggering blow, Arbogast's shocking murder. And the ending!

I don't intend to retell the entire plot, but I thought you might be interested to hear how gullible I was, how readily I'd played the marionette to Mr. Hitchcock's puppeteer.

It took several viewings before I fully comprehended the depth, the layers of Psycho. *And even when I reran it a few times prior to beginning this book, I discovered elements I had missed before. (I want you to know, I've rewritten this chapter several times to keep current with my changing perceptions.) I have found that not just* Psycho, *but many of Hitchcock's works, hold secrets to ferret out.* Psycho, *however, is probably the film most studied.*

And perhaps the most striking symbolism in Psycho *is Hitchcock's repeated use of mirrors and windows. There are more than a dozen examples of double images, hammering into our subconscious again and again the duality of good and bad, the split personality that lives to some degree in us all.*

- The blinds' shadows cutting John's face and mine as we look out the window in the opening scene in the hotel room.
- Mirrors in Marion's home reflecting her as she packs. (Also in the background, a bathroom with the same shower configuration as in the motel.)
- Hitchcock shooting through the windshield of Marion's car.
- Her looking in the rearview mirror of the car.
- Marion's counting out the money in the used car dealer's rest room in front of the mirror.
- The policeman's mirrored glasses.
- Tony's and my reflections in the window on the porch of the motel.
- Hitchcock shooting through the glass telephone booth to show Arbogast on the phone to Sam and Lila.

Shadows were another tool Hitchcock used to tweak our psyche.

- The shadow of Marion precedes her in the real estate office and in her home while she is packing, leading the audience, telegraphing that something unexpected is going to happen.
- Mother is seen only in shadows until the very end.
- While Marion eats and Tony talks in the motel's back room, his shadow is ominously outlined on the wall before the lens reaches his face.
- Shadows of the stuffed birds loom menacingly over Marion while she daintily chews her sandwich.
- At the swamp, with tree limbs all around him, Tony's outline is birdlike, and his hands clawlike, as he munches candy corn.
- At the hardware store, backlighting causes rakes to appear as talons on a bird, poised above Vera Miles's head.

We've dealt with mirrors and glass and shadows. But we can't forget about water signals.

- Does the heavy rainfall foreshadow the shower?
- Does the abating of the rain indicate Marion's inner tranquillity after her courageous decision? And does it also forecast the lull before the real storm hits Marion?

Food for thought.

The double entendre of the word "bird" in regard to Psycho *has been discussed at great length in other books, but I would be remiss not to at least touch on this.*

Again, Mr. Hitchcock and the rich dialogue of Stefano and Bloch gave us the two sides, demonstrating further our divided souls.

- What was Marion's last name?
  Crane.
- Where did Marion Crane live?
  Phoenix (the name of a legendary bird that is consumed in fire by its own act, and rises in youthful freshness from its ashes).
- In England, a slang word for a young girl is—Bird.
- What did Norman Bates do for a hobby?
  He stuffed birds.
- Where did Marion sit when she had a bite?
  On a sofa in front of a wall where stuffed birds were hung.
- What did Norman say while Marion was eating her food?
  "You eat like a bird."
- What was Norman's last name?
  Bates. And don't you "bait" birds?
- What did Norman say people do, when he lashed out at Marion for suggesting an institution for Mother?
  ". . . cluck their thick tongues and shake their heads . . ."

Joseph Stefano: "We used to meet every day for about four weeks, just to talk about things. He mentioned something about mirrors and stuff. Then he mentioned them again later on. It was so typical of Hitchcock that if he liked something visually he wanted to do it more.

"I said to him one day, 'You're talking about a reprise from the mirror scene.'

"He said, 'Yes, . . . reprise, yes.'

"My background was music and musical comedy, and when you sing the song again, it is a reprise. He loved the idea of calling it a reprise."

As long as we're on the subject of why one must see Hitchcock's films more than once, specifically Psycho, we have to talk about one of the movie's least obvious elements, the sprinklings of humor he managed to mix into this horrifying thriller.

Actually, Hitchcock once playfully labeled Psycho a "black comedy." But, in all seriousness, he told Peggy Robertson, "I could never have made Psycho without a sense of humor."

The first small gag in the picture is both visual and traditional. Beginning with his first important film, The Lodger in 1926, Hitchcock had made silent cameo appearances. Audiences had come to look forward to these fleeting glimpses of the director, and he had to be careful they didn't get undue attention. Finally he decided, "I now make it a point to show up in the first five minutes so as to let the people look at the rest of the movie with no further distraction."

In Rebecca, he can be seen near a London phone booth occupied by George Sanders. He is leaving a pet store with a pair of dogs in The Birds. And in the most ingenious of his cameos, for the wartime drama Lifeboat (which featured only a handful of actors in the confined space of a small dinghy), Hitch was forced to appear in a newspaper photo as part of a before-and-after ad for a weight-loss product.

In Psycho, Hitchcock is seen in three-quarter profile standing in front of the real estate office as Marion rushes in following her

noontime rendezvous with Sam. He wears a cowboy hat, absolutely wrong for him (he could never be mistaken for a man of the Old West) but proper for the Arizona locale.

A few minutes later the swaggering oilman, with the $40,000 in cash, makes a pass at Marion, and her self-absorbed coworker (effectively played by Patricia Hitchcock) comes to Marion's desk and says, straight-faced, "He was flirting with you. I guess he must have noticed my wedding ring."

During the scene in the motel office, when Norman notices Marion picking at her food, he says, "You eat like a bird"; she glances around at the stuffed birds dominating the room, and says with a smile that softens the sarcasm, "You'd know, of course."

A touch of macabre humor surfaces in the moment when Marion's car halts for a second as it slips into the swamp ooze. A flitting expression of panic crosses Norman's face, and then subsides as the car suddenly starts its descent again. Strangely, this never fails to cause nervous giggles in the audience, then sighs of collective relief when the car finally completely disappears. At this point, Norman has won our sympathy; we are rooting for him to succeed in covering up Mother's dreadful deed.

As Arbogast, Marty Balsam gets to deliver an amusing non sequitur: After being told by Sam and Lila that apparently no one in Fairvale has spotted Marion and her stolen money, Arbogast replies, "Someone always sees a girl with forty thousand dollars."

I think the strangest line of dialogue in the film is not so much humorous as peculiar. Sam and Lila rouse Sheriff Chambers and his wife to seek help after Arbogast has apparently disappeared. Chambers listens, and then explains that Arbogast couldn't possibly have questioned Norman's mother, as she's been dead for ten years. Mrs. Chambers volunteers, "I helped Norman pick out the dress she was buried in—periwinkle blue." This remark was delivered with such earnestness by the wonderful Lurene Tuttle that it took on a momentary import, which led some viewers to speculate if "periwinkle blue" played some significant role in the mystery. A possible red herring?

This section is meant to be about the release of *Psycho*. But when one is writing about a man as complicated as Alfred Hitchcock, and a movie like *Psycho*, it is easy to take a seemingly simple path and have it turn into a freeway.

I did less promotional publicity for *Psycho* than for any other feature I ever made. That's quite amazing, considering the impact the picture made on the world. But I believe Mr. Hitchcock did *more* public relations on it than on any of his previous or subsequent films. And I think I know the reasons for both of these rather odd facts.

First, Hitch didn't want Tony or me to make the usual rounds of television, radio, and print interviews, because we might have spilled the beans about the contents of the plot. It was vital to the success of the movie that it maintain its surprise value. And Tony and I could have easily blurted out giveaway answers to someone's sneaky questions. Mr. Hitchcock was accustomed to sparring with the media—relished the challenge, I bet. He must have had the time of his life jousting with reporters over *Psycho*. They were probably pulling their hair out, but he was unflappable.

The trailer he shot for the film is a classic. No one could do Hitchcock better than Hitchcock. You could just see a wicked little smile skulking behind that angelic, innocent face as he personally conducted a leisurely tour of the Bates Motel and the family's Victorian house, hinting dryly at the gruesome mayhem audiences could expect from his latest opus. You knew he was having fun with you but you couldn't help yourself—you swallowed the hook anyway. This meandering preview did not contain a single scene from the film and concluded with a close-up of a screaming Vera Miles (wearing a short wig that looked like my hair style).

Hitchcock admitted later that this final shot was a cheat, but he felt it was justified. He had to obscure both Vera's and my roles. The subterfuge extended even further to some of the eight-by-ten photos released to newspapers to promote the picture. The caption on one shot of Vera even indicated that *she* meets a violent end. Naughty, naughty Hitch!

Second, I believe Mr. Hitchcock gave 110 percent of himself during the selling of *Psycho* because he couldn't stand to have Paramount proven right. Paramount was distributing the film, but they had passed on participating in the making of the movie. The mysterious "they" at the studio didn't have faith in the material at all. Plus, in their opinion, this was not the type of Hitchcock fare that would produce the box-office magic his other projects had. So, Mr. Hitchcock financed it himself, through his company, Shamley Productions, and decided to shoot it at Universal Studios under the Revue television unit. I have to imagine that Hitchcock was determined to do everything, and then some, to ensure *Psycho*'s triumph. In the beginning, I doubt he realized how far his efforts and the picture itself would travel.

In 1964, Hitchcock turned over all his outstanding stock in Shamley Productions to Universal's parent company, Music Corporation of America. In 1968, Paramount relinquished distribution and all other financial rights to Psycho *as well. Mr. Hitchcock's six films after* Psycho *also were produced and distributed through the auspices of Universal.*

His insistence that theaters not allow any person to be admitted once the picture had started was ground-breaking and caused quite a ruckus! That had never been done before except for road-show sagas when they had two showings a day. Before *Psycho* a ticket buyer could go into a movie at any time, in the middle of the first film of a double feature, for instance, see the rest of that picture, the next one all the way through, and then leave at the scene in the first movie during which he or she had come in.

This policy did not, as some critics claimed, stem from Hitchcock's desire to establish a publicity-grabbing gimmick. It was something he had given much thought to, even as he was still in the midst of production.

Peggy Robertson: "One day after we had finished shooting, I was sitting in his office at Paramount, and he said, 'You know, it worries me that anyone who comes in the theater late will be waiting to see Janet Leigh. And we've already killed her. They'll be waiting all through the picture for Janet to appear. Something should be done about that!'

"And I said, 'Well, what could be done about it?'

"He replied, 'Well, people shouldn't be allowed in the movie house after the picture has started.'

"And that's how the whole thing came about!"

And so was born the most effective—and controversial—policy any Hollywood promotional campaign had ever had. The theater owners sent up a cry that could be heard around the world. They would lose their customers! No one would wait outside if there were empty seats inside! This could cause riots! They would lose their shirts!

But Hitchcock was adamant. And so the owners mumbled and grumbled, but they complied. The opening day brought calls from frustrated exhibitors all over. "It's the nine A.M. show and the theater is only half full and there are hundreds of people outside! Please, can I let them in?"

Absolutely no way! So the managers moaned and groaned and hung up, angry as hell.

But what they didn't realize was that once the public found out the studio was serious about "seeing it from the beginning," they would line up so they would be sure to get in for the next showing. Soon there were no more half-empty movie houses and theater owners were capitalizing on the very policy they had denounced. If it rained, they provided umbrellas. There were even chairs provided (which cost extra) for comfort while waiting.

People tried every trick in the book to break the rule. Reporters, eager for a good story, hired pregnant women to beg theater managers to "just let me in, because of my condition, you know. I won't tell anybody." But the men in charge held their ground. They very politely offered refuge—in their offices, but not inside their movie houses. Hitchcock was proclaimed a champion, a pioneer in presentation. The in-studio magazine *Paramount World* wrote, "Right now, the exhibitors showing *Psycho* are the happiest showmen in the whole wide world. They want to embrace Hitchcock, compliment Paramount, and thank their lucky stars at having booked *Psycho*."

It's difficult for us to envision why there was such an uproar, because Hitchcock's way is the norm today. But trust me, it happened.

The Hitchcocks journeyed to most of the United States—in fact, to most parts of the globe. And they received a hero's welcome everywhere they went. In Australia, for example, their visit caused the greatest publicity and public interest of anyone who had arrived on those shores, excepting royalty, in that country's history. Indeed, by 1960, Alfred Hitchcock was the most famous director in the world, having handily supplanted the venerable Cecil B. DeMille, whose fame dated back to the silent era. Hitch was, in fact, as recognizable as any of the superstars in his many films.

The film broke all box-office records in the United States, Canada, China, Britain, Asia, France, Japan, and all of South America. Hitchcock and *Psycho* had definitely swept the world off its collective feet.

I just gave you the good news; now for the bad. *Psycho* was not critically acclaimed at first; the reviews were mixed, about 60 percent negative and 40 percent positive.

Time magazine: "Director Hitchcock bears down too heavily in this one, and the delicate illusion of reality necessary for a creak-and-shriek movie becomes, instead, a spectacle of stomach-churning horror."

Newsweek magazine: "*Psycho* is plainly a gimmick movie, whose suspense depends on a single, specific twist . . . climactic scenes are rather standardly spooky and contrived . . . milked every drop of excitement from the early stretch—aided and abetted by fine performances from Perkins and Leigh, and from a shot of a showerhead squirting directly down into the camera, this stunt gets more scare into the film than the entire Victorian mansion."

New York Times: ". . . a blot on an honorable career . . . slowly paced for Mr. Hitchcock and given over to a lot of detail."

New York Daily News: "The suspense builds up slowly but surely to an almost unbearable pitch of excitement. Anthony Perkins's performance is the best of his career . . . Janet Leigh

Volume 6, Numbers 7,8   July-August, 1960

film; c) The unique, 10-minute special film in which Hitchcock himself conducts the viewer 'backstage' of "Psycho" and which of its own accord is virtually worth the price of admission (and which also must be seen from the beginning); and finally d) The pair of backbone-rasping, and interest-compelling, trailers which demand that the viewer see "Psycho" at the very earliest moment — and see it from the start.

The foregoing is but a segment of the overpowering (and completely commendable) job of merchandising of "Psycho" which, under the inspiration of Mr. Weltner, has been done by Jerome Pickman, Martin Davis and their tinglingly-alert aides both in Home Office and in the Studio.

Plus, of course, the shadowy, sinister figure of Alfred Hitchcock lurking in the background, a cherubic look on his face, but a poised dagger for the hindmost.

PPPPPPPPPPPPPP

IT IS REQUIRED THAT YOU SEE

PSYCHO

FROM THE VERY BEGINNING!

The next showing of **PSYCHO** *begins at __*

The manager of this theatre has been instructed, at the risk of his life, not to admit to the theatre any persons after the picture starts.

Any spurious attempts to enter by side doors, fire escapes, or ventilating shafts will be met by force.

The entire objective of this extraordinary policy, of course, is to help you enjoy PSYCHO more.

This is one of the key components in the See-It-From-the-Start showmanship campaign which has catapulted Alfred Hitchcock's "Psycho" into the ranks of the industry's all-time successes. It is the lobby standee which is being supplied to every theatre booking "Psycho." It is a vital controlling factor in making sure that no one - and positively no one - sees "Psycho" other than from the very beginning.

PPFPPPPPPPPPP

PERFECTION IN SHOWMANSHIP SUPPORT has been achieved for "Psycho" to a degree never before attained by any other Paramount picture. These showmanship tools have come from four unprecedented sources, and they are pure, shining gold for the procuring of towering box-office returns the world over.

The four ace aids are: a) A press-book on film demonstrating the irrefutable power of the policy of having the picture seen from the beginning only, by the process of admitting no one to the theatre after the main title has flashed; b) A special trailer in which George Weltner, as Paramount Pictures vice-president in charge of world sales, personally introduces four representative exhibitors and has them individually tell of their unparalleled successful experiences with the Hitchcock

has never been better." (Hooray for Wanda Hale, certainly the critic of my choosing!)

Esquire magazine: ". . . merely one of those television shows padded out to two hours by adding pointless subplots and realistic detail . . . a reflection of a most unpleasant mind, a mean, sly sadistic little mind."

Village Voice: ". . . first American movie since *Touch of Evil* to stand in the same creative rank as the great European films."

This last review was of particular interest to me as I starred in both Psycho *and* Touch of Evil. *In 1962, another picture in which I appeared,* Manchurian Candidate, *was placed in the same glorified category.*

New York Herald Tribune: ". . . rather difficult to be amused at the forms insanity may take . . . keeps your attention like a snake-charmer."

STUNNING SUCCESS OF "PSYCHO" IS TRU ALLIANCE OF GREAT PRODUCTION AND PENETRATING SHOWMANSHIP

BOSTON - When Alfred Hitchcock was circuiting the United States recently in the interests of "Psycho," he was a proverbial 'jack of all trades.' Here he is assisting Arthur Morton,manager of the Paramount Theatre,in the placing of a title of a certain super-successful picture.

"P S Y C H O" has impacted London. (see Page 13)
Japan, inSeptember, and Australia, in October, will be the next countries to reel under the Hitchcock impact.

Supervising the international movements of "Psycho" from New York will be Milton Goldstein, who adds these duties to those of "The Ten Commandments," "The Greatest Show on Earth" and "Samson and Delilah."

OMAHA - The Orpheum had a whiz of a "Psycho"-line also — it went practically around the block. And just in case someone didn't know what it was all about - there was a sign. ➤

PRESENTATION MEETINGS
(Continued from P. 3)

of 400 exhibitors from New York and adjoining states, as well as from Canada, the participants were treated to the precedental novelty of a press book "on film," plus filmed tributes from exhibitors testifying to the merits of the policy of "no admissions after start of the film"; also a film showing the actual working of the policy at the DeMille Theatre in New York City. Additional films comprised the two "Psycho" trailer, plus the 6½ minute special film starring Mr. Hitchcock himself on the sets of the picture.

(This special film is being made available abroad with Mr. Hitchcock speaking in French, German, Italian and several other languages).

The ample showing of the dynamic showmanship films was supported by presentations made by Messrs Weltner and Fickman, and by Hugh Owen, vice-president of Paramount Film Distributing Corp. and Eastern sales manager.

Nothing was spared in making available to exhibitors as possible aids in introducing the new "See-It-From-the-Start" policy on "Psycho." Pressbooks, sales manuals, radio and trailer tapes, standees, lobby displays — all were described by the speakers, and their availability stressed.

Paramount's president, Barney Balaban and Adolph Zukor, chairman of the board, attended the meeting.

Similar meetings were later held in Chicago, Atlanta, Dallas and Los Angeles. These have been reported on elsewhere in this issue.

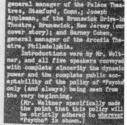

The Policy....

Powerfully and unqualifiedly supporting Mr. Weltner's statement of policy were four eminent exhibitors, all of whom have felt the titanic box-office power of Alfred Hitchcock's "Psycho." The four were Walter Reade,Jr., president of Walter Reade Theatres (which includ New York's DeMille); Melvin Miller general manager of the Palace Theatres, Stamford, Conn.; Joseph Applemann, of the Brunswick Drive-In Theatre, Brunswick, New Jersey (our cover story); and Barney Cohen, general manager of the Arcadia Theatre, Philadelphia.

Introductions were by Mr. Weltner, and all five speakers conveyed with complete sincerity the dynamic power and the complete public acceptability of the policy of "Psycho" only (and always) being seen from the very beginning.

(Mr. Weltner especifically made the point that this policy will be strictly adhered to wherever "Psycho" is shown.)

You will find news of "Psycho" success on practically every page of this issue.
• • • • • • • • •

How Good is the "S.I.F.T.S." Policy?

You want to know how good is the "S.I.F.T.S." (See It From the Start) policy in connection with showings of "Psycho"? Then read this wire to Showmanship Manager Joe Friedman in New York from Mike Weiss, field representative in Philadelphia:

IN SPITE OF CONTINUOUS WARNINGS BY RADIO AND NEWSPAPER OF TURNADOWN AND TORRENTIAL DOWNPOUR OF RAIN, THE PEOPLE LINED THE BOARDWALK AND WAITED AT SCHEDULED HOURS TO SEE "PSYCHO" AT THE STRAND THEATRE IN WILDWOOD. THE BOARDWALK LINE EXTENDED FOR THE FIRST TIME IN THE HISTORY OF WILDWOOD TO THREE AND ONE HALF BLOCKS LONG ON THE OTHER SIDE OF THE BOX OFFICE. APPROXIMATELY 1,100 PEOPLE WAITED IN LINE. AUDIENCE REACTION AS USUAL WAS GREAT. THEATRE MANAGEMENT MOST EXCITED WITH THEIR POLICY AND ARE MOST WILLING TO SHOUT IT FROM THE ROOFTOPS.

(We have just noted that the initials

"Just a line" used to be just a phrase, an alibi for a brief note....But now, thanks to "Psycho" and its queues, "Just a line" is a national institution.

New York Daily Mirror: ". . . played out beautifully. . . [performances] were excellent . . . a scary startler, shake 'n' shock brand."

Meanwhile, Alfred Hitchcock's homecoming to England proved bittersweet. Although *Psycho* was shattering attendance records at the London Plaza Cinema, the British critics were savaging the film, the more stuffy ones openly questioning Hitchcock's taste, judgment, and yes, even his talent. Wow, when the critics turn, they *turn*.

There have been many theories advanced to explain Britain's crucifixions: Screenings held for the London press were mistimed and forced some critics to rush through their reviews to meet print deadlines; like their American counterparts, most of the

THE "PSYCHO" SHOWMANSHIP STORY WILL BE INSPIRING PRECEDENT FOR YEARS TO COME

HOLLYWOOD - Scene in Paramount's studio theatre as the "Psycho" showmanship presentation is made by Martin S. Davis, national director of advertising, publicity and showmanship. Meeting was attended by more than one hundred West Coast exhibitors, as well as by five Paramount branch managers and a number of members of the Los Angeles branch personnel.

ATLANTIC CITY - Sitters and standees - each had their own lines as the "See It From the Beginning" policy for "Psycho" was rigidly held at the Strand Theatre here. Of special significance was the fact that it cost extra money to sit (and wait) in the roll-chairs.

HOLLYWOOD - Mr. Hitchcock was very much in evidence at the studio showmanship meeting. Here he stands between Hamilton Fields (left), manager of the Iris Theatre in this city, and Jerry Shur, manager of the Golden Gate Theatre in Los Angeles.

NORTH BRUNSWICK, New Jersey - Police directing the overflow traffic at the Brunswick Drive-in, instructing the drivers to return for second showing of "Psycho." Traffic had backed up on U.S. Route #1 for distance of 1½ miles.

NORTH BRUNSWICK, New Jersey - A scream in the night was really that for the capacity car attendance at the Brunswick Drive-in, when "Psycho" shattered all precedents, all records, all attendances — and gave us our unique cover story for this issue.

WESTERN UNION TELEGRAM

WUCO65 PB281 P KYA019 DL PD

LONG BRANCH NJER JUNE 20 1050A EDT

GEORGE WELTNER

PARAMOUNT PICTURES CORP.

DEAR GEORGE, HOW THRILLING, HOW EXCITING, AFTER MY MANY YEARS IN ALL TYPES AND KINDS OF SHOWMANSHIP ACTIVITIES NEVER HAVE I HAD MORE PLEASURE THAN IN PARTICIPATING WITH YOU AND THE PARAMOUNT GANG IN THE RECORD BREAKING SHOWMANSHIP ENGAGEMENTS OF PSYCHO AT OUR DEMILLE AND BARONET THEATRES. MERCHANDISING ADVERTISING AND PROMOTIONAL CAMPAIGN HAS PULLED THE STOP FOR NEW YORK AND I AM SURE WILL DO LIKEWISE FOR THE REST OF THE COUNTRY. AGAIN MY CONGRATULATIONS TO WHAT I KNOW WILL BE A LONG RECORD SHATTERING ENGAGEMENT PSYCHO IS HITCHCOCKS MOST EXCITING SO FAR

WALTER READE JR.

Away back on June 20th, this was the New York telegram from Walter Reade, Jr. to George Weltner that really started the whole massive "Psycho" landslide. It has therefore been a supremely gratifying pleasure to see Mr. Reade's prophecy come so abundantly true.

Cover and other Brunswick Drive-in Pix by ED SULLIVAN

Many success stories have been written, but the success of PSYCHO is beyond all realm of belief.....When we discussed the 'admissions' plan with the exhibitor at the Scandia, he was very dubious......But what happened? People not only waited in line for the start of each performance, but they complimented the manager when they left the theatre for not having allowed them to enter during the screening....This policy sells tickets, definitely, through word-of-mouth advertising... The picture has played 6 weeks; it will go another 10, possibly 12.... On July 22 I met with 36 of the most influential exhibitors in this territory, representing 277 theatres. It was unanimously agreed that the 'admissions' policy would be used, and that the picture would be mingled-billed in both conventional and drive-in theatres...The staying power of the picture is without precedent. Extended playing time is the exception rather than the rule. Repeat bookings will equal and even exceed original bookings....All of this could not have been accomplished were it not for the foresight of Paramount and its advertising department, who gave us the ideas and the tools to do the job.

All over the nation the news about "Psycho" is jumping like a firecracker. Every branch has 'fantastic' reports to make — we put all the names in a hat — and Philadelphia's was drawn. Here are Ulrik Smith's highlights.

SUMMIT-SHATTERING "PSYCHO" SUCCESS KEYNOTES UNIQUE AND ENORMOUSLY EFFECTIVE SHOWMANSHIP PRESENTATION

In all of the glowing facets of show business nothing is so electrifying as box-office-success news. It outstrips the speed of light in reaching exhibitor consciousness; and it speeds with the flash rapidity of electrons in getting to executive consciousness.

Such is the situation with "P s y c h o" - the most electrifying triumph of producership and showmanship in a great many Paramount years. Success stories are pouring into 1501 Broadway at such a pace that if we were to record but a fraction of them, this publication would come out daily, and comprise 100 pages-plus each issue.

And they are not just commonplace success stories. Each and every box-office report is predicental, each and every one tells of receipts, records and raves far beyond all known accomplishments. Exhibitors who have had reservations regarding the policy of "no admissions after the start of the picture," who have demurred at a single-feature recommendation --- all of these men and women controlling theatres have, after the very first public screening, wanted to embrace Hitchcock, compliment Paramount, and thank their lucky stars at having booked "Psycho."

Right now, the exhibitors showing "Psycho" are the happiest showmen in the whole wide world.

NEW YORK - What was hailed by the principal speakers as "a new advance in pre-sellsmanship" was revealed by Paramount on July 19th at an exhibitor gathering at the DeMille Theatre which marked the opening of a series of five regional merchandising conferences on Alfred Hitchcock's "Psycho." Viewed by an estimated audience (turn to next page)

SATISFACTION AT MEETING's success is registered by three top-level attendees: (from left) Sam Rinzler, president of the Randforce Circuit;George Weltner, vice-president of Paramount Pictures Corp. in charge of world sales, and Harry Brandt, president of Brandt Theatres Corp.

SHOWMANSHIP IMPACT was delivered to the meeting by Jerry Pickman, Paramount Film Distribution Corp. vice-president in charge of advertising, publicity and showmanship.

MORE "PSYCHO" NEWS ON PAGES FOLLOWING

reviewers resented what they perceived as the exploitive tone of the film's promotion (photographs of audience members screaming and peering through their fingers in horror did little to endear the film to austere, cerebral film writers). And then, there was that lingering resentment by some in the British film community over what they saw as Hitchcock's abandonment of his homeland in favor of American success. When he left England in

1939 to make movies in Hollywood, he was considered Britain's most respected and successful film director. Then the first Hitchcock/Selznick collaboration, *Rebecca,* earned the Academy Award for Best Picture of 1940, and the Brits feared they had lost one of their premier film luminaries to Hollywood forever—and for all intents and purposes, they had.

But no matter—the Movie God had everything under control. Despite the British press drubbing, the public made *Psycho* the year's biggest hit.

Critics, who were used to VIP treatment from all the studios in all parts of the world, rebelled at the handling they received from Mr. Hitchcock. He did not allow exhibitors anywhere to have private screenings for reviewers. (This was in line with his "see it from the beginning" and secrecy platform. They might have given away the plot.) Instead they had to see the film with the regular paying public (they were given complimentary tickets, however) and sit through the shorts and coming attractions.

This no doubt miffed some of the prima donnas. But I disagreed with those who saw it as the reason for critics' less-than-great reactions to *Psycho.* I just thought that they were not prepared for a macabre movie from the man who had recently given them the elegant *To Catch a Thief* and *North by Northwest.* And, I think, the completely unprecedented innovations caught them by surprise, so they really weren't able to evaluate the film properly, at least not right away.

I don't know what prompted some critics to rereview *Psycho.* It might have been that the overwhelmingly positive public response caused them to think, "Maybe I had better take another look." Because the darn thing wouldn't go away; it wouldn't just lay down and die. No matter what they wrote, they couldn't kill it. It developed a life of its own and kept getting stronger and stronger. It was a true phenomenon.

At any rate, *Psycho* was given a second shot, and this time fared much better. Bosley Crowther of *The New York Times* included it on his Ten Best list of 1960. In 1966, *Time* magazine pronounced it "superlative" and "masterly." Sweet music to our ears!

The enormous international success of *Psycho* can partly be credited to the Hitchcocks' herculean efforts to promote it. I believe audiences the world over responded not only to its sensational aspects, but also to the obvious care and attention to detail found in its precise construction. It was clear to even the most unsophisticated filmgoer that *Psycho* was not to be confused with the cheapie "B" thrillers that were being churned out in large numbers.

In our explorations, we found a story about Anthony Perkins that was impossible to verify. I do hope it's true, because it shows my friend Tony's fine sense of humor. He was in Paris making a movie when *Psycho* was released. It was said he would hide outside theaters and when people filed out, their nerves frayed, Tony would abruptly leap from the shadows, wild-eyed, and shout at the crowd in his best Norman Bates style. Something those poor souls will likely never forget.

Oddly, a couple of strange objections were raised by censors in various countries. The majority of problems were connected to the shower murder, and Hitch did make some slight alterations to accommodate those complaints.

But in Britain, the censors wanted him to cut the shot of Norman washing blood off his hands after Marion's murder. And in Singapore, where apparently no one minded Marion's grisly demise, local Paramount officials were forced to delete the much less graphic stabbing of Arbogast, as well as a shot of Mother's corpse as Norman carries her downstairs. I guess every culture has its own little peculiarities.

Never did the critics or the members of the cast and crew think that thirty-five years later Psycho *would still be a potent force in this industry. That it would be dissected, studied, used as a textbook at universities. That I would still be receiving reams of mail from fans seven to seventy years old naming* Psycho *as one of their favorite films of all time.*

Here is a little trivia information for you. For the period ending 12/31/66, Psycho *had taken in fourteen million, three hundred thirty-two thousand, six hundred forty-eight dollars and ninety two cents ($14,332,648.92).*

Now take into consideration the fact that the average ticket price in 1960 was seventy-five cents ($0.75) as opposed to the seven to eight dollars it is now. By today's standards, the take would be up to one hundred thirty-three million, seven hundred seventy-one thousand dollars ($133,771,000.00).

Throw into the pot these figures: The world population in 1960 was roughly three billion people. In 1991 there were an estimated five and a half billion people. It would take a math major to explain the full implications of all this, but even I can see there were fewer possible ticket buyers in 1960. I can't even guess what Psycho's *final numbers would be today. I can say, though—not bad for a small black-and-white film that cost less than nine hundred thousand dollars ($900,000.00) to make.*

The fall of 1960 was dedicated to John F. Kennedy's quest for the presidency. That kickoff luncheon I mentioned earlier proved almost too successful—traffic jams tied up over half of Beverly Hills. Frank Sinatra, Dean Martin, the Peter Lawfords, Senator Ted Kennedy, and Tony Curtis and I were in attendance, and it really was a blockbuster. I became deputy registrar; I participated in political rallies all over California and even invaded some other states. Naturally, November 8 was a jubilant date for us, as John F. Kennedy was elected the thirty-fifth president of the United States.

The girls and I accompanied my husband Tony on location to the marine base at Camp Pendleton near Oceanside, California. He was shooting *The Outsiders,* and it was a beautiful spot for the children and me to enjoy.

"Janet is sure to be up for a supporting role in 'PSYCHO'!"
—LOUELLA PARSONS

"Janet Leigh will win the Academy Oscar for her startling performance in 'PSYCHO'!"
—JIMMY STARR

"Best supporting actress, Janet Leigh for 'PSYCHO'!"
—FEDERATED WOMEN'S CLUBS OF AMERICA

"Janet Leigh, never better!"
—NEW YORK DAILY NEWS

"Miss Leigh is tremendous!"
—BOSTON GLOBE

"Janet Leigh is superb!"
—SYDNEY, AUSTRALIA, SUNDAY TRUTH

"Miss Leigh is excellent!"
—HOLLYWOOD REPORTER

Our own little mystery: Pick out the non sequitur quote.

Warren Cowan, head of the PR firm Rogers and Cowan, which Tony and I both used, made the trip down to urge me to make a bid for an Academy Award nomination for *Psycho* in the Best Actress category.

I looked at him as if he were mad. "Are you nuts? I'm only in the first third of the picture," I told him. "No possible way! Anyhow, I'm too scared."

He insisted, "Then at least for Best Supporting Actress."

I said I'd think about it. When I returned to Los Angeles, Lew Wasserman and Warren Cowan and I had a confab.

Normally, Lew was quiet about anything relating to publicity, but this time he was not. "I think you should. Hitch thinks you should. The picture is an undisputed box-office champ, and your contribution certainly warrants recognition."

Mr. Hitchcock, known for his thriftiness, offered to foot the bill for two ads in the trade papers. Well, what did I have to lose—besides a little security, a little pride, and a little dent in my protective armor! Okay, I agreed, Rogers and Cowan could go forward with the advertisements.

INTERMISSION

As Janet mentioned, *Psycho* encountered several international censorship hurdles, but the first and most crucial one it faced was in Hollywood.

"After George Tomasini put together one of the first rough cuts of the film," Peggy Robertson recalls, "Hitch said, 'We better get it over to Luigi.'"

Luigi Luraschi was Paramount's liaison with the still-powerful Motion Picture Association of America, an industry-wide self-censorship board that had been established in the early thirties by former Postmaster General Will H. Hays. The Hays Office, which had evolved into the MPAA, was founded in part as a response to what was perceived as the glorification of crime kingpins in the gritty Warner's gangster films and to counteract the so-called loosening of sexual mores, as exemplified by the racy comedies of Jean Harlow and the candid double entendres Mae West spouted so amusingly. (Several real-life Hollywood scandals also contributed to the establishment of the Hays Office.)

The code directives, followed rigidly by the studios, were designed to protect youthful American moviegoers from any form of moral transgression. It was essential that in the movies, punishment was dealt out to all who committed crimes, no sex was depicted outside marriage—and very little within—and certainly no one was ever seen nude. And forget any story line dealing, even obliquely, with homosexuality or miscegenation.

Although MPAA code strictures had frequently been successfully challenged during the latter half of the fifties, Hitchcock knew he was tempting the wrath of the board with several real (and implied) elements of *Psycho*. But he was well prepared for Luigi Luraschi when he screened the movie for him at Paramount.

"I was sitting next to Luigi," says Peggy Robertson, "and he began shifting around in his seat as Janet undressed in the motel bathroom. 'Anything the matter, Luigi?' asked Hitch dryly. And then on came the shower scene. By now, Luigi is shaking with fear and he shouts, 'Hitch! I see a breast!' and Hitch replied calmly, 'Luigi, it's all in your imagination. There are no breasts in this picture. Are there, Peggy?'"

Despite Hitch's assurances, Luraschi insisted on showing the shower scene to other members of the MPAA board, half of whom felt they had indeed seen a naked Janet Leigh. Hitch agreed "to take out the nudity," but simply returned the scene, untouched, to the board a few days later. Now the members flip-flopped, to a man; those who had seen nudity before were now satisfied that it had been deleted, while others now saw nudity that they hadn't spotted before.

The situation was finally resolved, with the result that the shower murder remained exactly as Hitch had filmed it minus the one "offensive" buttocks shot. Ultimately, he struck a bargain with the board: Luraschi and his cohorts had also objected to the film's sexy opening with Janet and John Gavin, so Hitch, according to script supervisor Marshall Schlom, told the MPAA, "If you leave the shower sequence as is, I will reshoot the opening, but I want you people on the set to tell me how you will pass it, as you watch it." Schlom adds, "We scheduled a reshoot, but they never showed up, so we never shot it. And finally they agreed they didn't see nudity in the shower scene sequence."

Never one to toss compliments around freely to his collaborators, Hitchcock was content to take most of the credit for *Psycho*'s tremendous success.

"I don't care about the acting," he told François Truffaut in reference to *Psycho* in a 1967 interview. "But I do care about the pieces of film and the photography and the sound track and all of the technical ingredients that made the audience scream . . . it wasn't a message that stirred the audiences, nor was it a great performance . . . they were aroused by pure film."

Of course, Hitch did care about the acting, as he did every tiny detail of his films. This minimizing of his cast's contributions to *Psycho* seems shortsighted. Surely Hitchcock must have realized that the superb performances of his leads contributed enormously to the brilliance of the film.

Anthony Perkins's Norman is not only the role for which he is best remembered (particularly since he re-created it in three *Psycho* sequels), it stands on its own as a masterly example of movie acting at its most skillful. His Norman is charming, helpful, concerned, and downright sweet when he first encounters Marion. He is, in fact appealing enough for audiences (who see the film for the first time), to imagine that a romance might develop between him and the attractive young woman checking into his motel.

Perkins allows us to see a strong indication of Norman's troubled dark side when he later harangues Marion in response to her suggestion that his mother might be better off in an institution. Also, his awkward bumblings when confronted by a suspicious Arbogast is a classic example of faulty lying techniques in the face of authority. Later, when Norman climbs the stairs of the Bates house to bring his mother's remains down to the cellar, his gait as he walks up the staircase is just the slightest bit swishy. Was Tony offering a subtle hint regarding his character's sexuality? His final scene in the prison cell, played only with facial expressions accompanying an inner monologue, tops off the movie in a striking, unsettling way.

Janet is no less riveting in a role that couldn't have seemed nearly so interesting on paper. Her Marion is painted in subtle strokes that invite the audience to read between the lines of her character and motivations. Like Norman, she is a keeper of secrets, and while we learn early of one of them—her illicit love affair with Sam—we get no hint of her intentions to steal her bosses's money when she complains of a headache and asks for the afternoon off. Janet never telegraphs Marion's larcenous impulse; we believe completely that she is a trusted employee who fully intends to drop the $40,000 off at the bank before going home to rest.

Yet, when we see that Marion *is* planning to abscond with the money, we are not terribly surprised, thanks to the artful way Janet has set up a complex character—and in a remarkably brief amount of screen time.

The scene in which Marion eats a simple meal prepared by Norman in the dreary office of the Bates Motel is one that, in less talented hands, might have come off as simply talky and expository. As acted by Janet and Tony, however, it is one of the finest two-character scenes in any Hitchcock film. As Norman expounds on subjects ranging from the eating habits of birds to taxidermy and his mother's mental condition, Marion listens attentively and sympathizes with him, while at the same time making up her mind about her own dilemma.

With a minimum of dialogue, Janet has been able to convey exactly what Marion is thinking. She doesn't simply listen impassively to Perkins's dialogue; she digests it intellectually and emotionally, and then shares her reaction with the audience by allowing her feelings to play gently across her face. By the time we are told aloud by Marion that she has decided to return to Phoenix to extricate herself from the "private trap" she is in, we already know of her intentions, in large part because of the way she has responded to Norman's conversation.

Really *listening* to your fellow actor and reacting in a seemingly genuine manner—as if you've never heard his or her dialogue before—is one of the most basic acting tenets. Yet certain performers are more adept at it than others. Janet's talent in this area is evident in almost all of her movies, but she utilizes it with special aplomb in *Psycho*.

And while Janet has talked about the unique technical challenges the shower murder presented, her performance in this most famous of all film scenes must be remarked upon as well.

"She did an amazing job with that horrifying scene," says Lillian Sidney. "When you think of all the distractions she was facing and how the scene had to be shot in such piecemeal fashion, it's a real sign of her professionalism that she was able to retain such a high degree of concentration." Robert Bloch said he found Janet to be "the best one in the picture. . . . I wish I had written the character as well as she played her."

For all of the "pure film" techniques Hitchcock so proudly employed for *Psycho*, the enduring popularity of the picture must also be credited to the dynamic performances of its actors. And what is "pure film" anyway if not brilliant on-screen acting?

C.N.

1961:
THE RESULT

Bringing in this new year was a rather tame affair. Those of us connected to the Kennedys were saving up our energy for the real celebration that was to take place in three weeks in Washington, D.C. We were in the planning stages of the Presidential Gala, so our heads were buried deep in the sands of rehearsals.

The January 13 cover of *Life* put a damper on our spirits, however. It was a picture of Clark Gable from *The Misfits*—he had just died, and it was the last film he made. He was such a giant! Life could be so unpredictable. Who would ever—*ever*—have thought that Marilyn Monroe, Gable's young costar in that movie, would grace a special-edition *Life* cover—an issue dedicated to her death—only a year and a half later.

I was one of the many celebrities who flew on a chartered plane to perform in the January 19 Presidential Gala and to attend the January 20 Inauguration and the numerous Inaugural Balls. Someone cracked, "If this plane crashes, the entertainment business is through!" (My husband, Tony, did not fly; he took the train.)

New York luminaries joined the Western contingent, and this is a partial list of the assembled stars (talk about name-dropping): Leonard Bernstein, Gene Kelly, Milton Berle, Nat "King" Cole, Harry Belafonte, Fredric March, Juliet Prowse, Ethel Merman, Jimmy Durante, Alan King, Keely Smith, Louis Prima, Bette

Davis, Joey Bishop, Helen Traubel, Ella Fitzgerald, Frank Sinatra. And, of course, there were the D.C. notables, topped by the brightest stars of all, President Kennedy and his First Lady.

What a hassle! We all rehearsed in the afternoon, planning to return to our hotel to change and get all gussied up before the 9:00 P.M. curtain. But Mother Nature put a damper on our arrangements, as Washington was hit by one of the worst blizzards in years. Traffic was almost at a standstill, and there was no way any of us could make the round-trip in time. My hairdresser had flown in from New York and was at the hotel, so I called him and he became our hero. He went into as many rooms as possible and picked up gowns and shoes and hairpieces and underwear and tuxedos and shirts and cuff links and etc., etc., etc., etc. When he arrived at the Washington Armory, his group (he had commandeered some assistants) looked as if they were preparing for a fashion show. Which, in a way, I guess they were.

So, some of us were able to wear our glad rags. Unfortunately, not everyone fared as well. I remember Ethel Merman and Bette Davis had to do the evening performance in their street clothes. (They were so great, no one could have cared less.)

Naturally the show started late, because President and Mrs. Kennedy were delayed, as was most of the audience. The gala was a sellout, which meant the money was in, but still we wanted a full auditorium for this tribute to our new president. Thank goodness, once we were over the hurdle of the storm, the evening was a smash.

An ironic twist: On the plane to Washington, D.C., I finished reading the novel *Manchurian Candidate*. Not realizing the tragedy it foresaw. Not knowing Frank Sinatra would buy the rights to the movie and star in it. Not aware I would be a costar.

The festivities didn't stop—not that we were in a hurry for them to end. We saw the investiture of Robert Kennedy as attorney general of the United States, followed by a luncheon at Hickory Hill (Ethel and Robert Kennedy's estate). Then Jean Kennedy and Steve Smith, Ambassador Joseph Kennedy, Pat Kennedy and Peter Lawford, Leonard Gershe, Roger Edens, and the two of us boarded the family plane, the *Caroline,* for a week of fun in Palm Beach, Florida, as guests of Ambassador and Mrs. Joseph Kennedy.

The albums I have from these trips belong in a museum, but I couldn't part with them. The photos capture the spirit, the idealism, the unabashed devotion the country felt toward the president. The union was truly united. We were all for one and he was one for all.

The only event that could even approach that experience happened on February 27, 1961. The four of us were relaxing at our Palm Springs, California, house. Tony was playing golf with Frank Sinatra, the children were napping, and I was reading by the pool. The telephone rang, and I rushed to pick it up so it wouldn't wake the girls.

John Foreman, of Rogers and Cowan, spoke each word very slowly, carefully, deliberately. "Janet, you have just been nominated for an Academy Award!"

I wish, that in describing my reaction, I could do justice to how I felt. I was so *full.* I was so *grateful.* I felt so *blessed.* I had a healthy family, I had been given such wondrous opportunities, and now to be rewarded like *this.* To be one of five actresses picked out of thousands of talented ladies! Incredible!

After I absorbed the shock of my great good fortune, I was eager to hear more good news about *Psycho.* Alfred Hitchcock was nominated for Best Director. John L. Russell was nominated for Cinematography (Black and White), and Joseph Hurley and Robert Clatworthy were nominated for Art Direction—Set Decoration (Black and White).

I kept waiting for one more name and thought maybe John was teasing me. But he said that was all there was. Not possible!

How could Anthony Perkins's sensitive, masterful performance not be acknowledged? As happy as I was for me, I was greatly disappointed for Tony. Trevor Howard (*Sons and Lovers*), Burt Lancaster (*Elmer Gantry),* Jack Lemmon *(The Apartment)*, Laurence Olivier (*The Entertainer*), and Spencer Tracy (*Inherit the Wind)* were all deserving of the honor, all superb artists. But so was Anthony Perkins.

I wish I had had the presence of mind to send a wire to Tony that was similar to the one Hitch sent. It read, "I am ashamed of your fellow actors."

I don't think my reactions were due solely to my association with *Psycho* and the people involved; I trust my motives were based on merit. Not only was Tony snubbed, but I firmly believe Joseph Stefano deserved a nomination for Writing, Martin Balsam for Supporting Actor, and, absolutely, Bernard Herrmann for his dramatic Scoring.

I've stewed about these oversights for years. I'm glad I finally have this podium, so to speak, and a captive audience to whom I can air my feelings publicly. I am pleased to report to you, however, that on January 12, 1961, Tony Perkins won Best Actor in a tie with Richard Attenborough in an award given by the International Board of Motion Picture Reviewers, based in London.

The English named Psycho *Best Film in a tie with* The Angry Silence. *(And these came after the scalding British reviews.)*

When the list of nominees for the Academy Awards was printed, they were as follows:

SUPPORTING ACTRESS

Glynis Johns, *The Sundowners*

Shirley Jones, *Elmer Gantry*

Shirley Knight, *Dark at the Top of the Stairs*

Janet Leigh, *Psycho*

Mary Ure, *Sons and Lovers*

(Seeing it in print, I still couldn't believe it)

DIRECTION

Jack Cardiff, *Sons and Lovers*

Jules Dassin, *Never on Sunday*

Alfred Hitchcock, *Psycho*

Billy Wilder, *The Apartment*

Fred Zinnemann, *The Sundowners*

CINEMATOGRAPHY (BLACK AND WHITE)

The Apartment, Joseph La Shelle

The Facts of Life, Charles B. Lang, Jr.

Inherit the Wind, Ernest Laszlo

Psycho, John L. Russell

Sons and Lovers, Freddie Francis

ART DIRECTION—SET DECORATION (BLACK AND WHITE)

The Apartment, Alexander Trauner; Edward G. Boyle

The Facts of Life, Joseph McMillan Johnson and Kenneth A. Reid; Ross Dowd

Psycho, Joseph Hurley and Robert Clatworthy; George Milo

Sons and Lovers, Tom Morahan; Lionel Couch

Visit to a Small Planet, Hal Pereira and Walter Tyler;

Sam Comer and Arthur Krams

Looking at all these names, I realized what excellent company we were in. The competition was awesome. But whatever the outcome, we'd come this far; no one could take that away from us.

I have another correction for the record. A quote was attributed to me in one of the other Psycho *or* Hitchcock *books regarding my nomination. I was reported to have said, "I think I have just as good a chance as any of the other girls." It's not a big deal, except I didn't say it. I would never have been that presumptuous or cocky. I never have been, it just isn't my way of thinking. Actually, because I was thrust into this profession rather abruptly, I have always felt I was playing catch-up, trying to learn everything so quickly. I have often undergone bouts of feeling inadequate, so I know I harbored no illusion about being equal to that distinguished collection of actresses. I knew I was lucky as hell to have squeaked in at all.*

The telegrams and notes of congratulations were overwhelming. They were not only from close associates and bosom buddies, but from unexpected sources as well. I am going to have you take part in the reading of some of this special correspondence.

I'll begin with Exhibit A. Joseph Stefano wrote a beautiful letter when he saw the finished print of *Psycho.*

March 30, 1960
Dear Janet:
Yesterday I saw the completed, scored and titled version of "Psycho." It is an impressive picture. In many respects, a strange and rather haunting picture. I think it will be a fine suc-

cess. And, I think, too, that your performance in it is one of the most expert screen performances I've ever seen. What you have done is so much more than mere acting. You've created a person, a live and touching and extremely moving person, and I believe it is your interpretation of Marion Crane that gives the picture a dimension which extends it somewhat outside the bounds of the usual motion picture. I knew when I saw a few of the rushes that you were building something high and shining; the completed picture proves it. Because of the girl you created, the murder of that girl becomes a thing less of horror and more of tragedy. I almost wanted to sigh, "No, stop it," when you were being slain. I was so brought into your world of Marion Crane that I wanted her to go back and return the money and correct and rectify her mistake. My wife told me that in the midst of her horrified reaction to the murder in the shower, she began to cry. She was crying for a girl you made real to her. You are to be congratulated and, especially by an author, loved for your work. Thank you, dear, for being one of the prime reasons why I am proud of "Psycho."

Sincerely, Joe

Then he followed with this after the nomination:

March 1, 1961
Dear Janet:
My congratulations on your nomination. It was so right and so deserved. As I told you when I first saw the finished picture, your performance caught my breath and gave me the satisfaction a writer knows only when a deep, fine and thinking actor plays a role he has written. I hope you win the award; it could go to no finer example of expert and exciting picture acting. And I hope we'll be associated again, soon.

Love and Best Wishes,
Joe

What more could any actress ask! His words were like precious drops of water to someone in a desert of blazing uncertainty. I told Joe when I interviewed him for this book how I have treasured those messages.

Joseph Stefano: "I have always felt that you held the picture together. I had this feeling, I said to someone, that the moment you came on the screen, it was like you had plucked a string on a violin, and that tremor kept going and going and going, even after your character was slain, it just kept going throughout the picture!"

My wonderful Tony (Perkins) sent two sweet telegrams. He never said one word about his own lack of a nomination, but he had to feel let down. Nonetheless, he was thoughtful to me.

Congratulations. Hope you get the award too.
Love,
Tony Perkins

What did I keep telling you?
Love,
Tony P.

Natalie Wood and husband Robert Wagner sent a funny one.

When you say thank you (for the Oscar) don't forget your name is Mrs. Corrine Corfu.
Love,
Nat and R.J.

When I was going through all my memorabilia for research and I came across this wire, I couldn't remember who Corrine Corfu was. I called R.J., and together we resurrected the mean-

ing. At the time, the raging album was Mel Brooks's "2,000-Year-Old Man." And somewhere in his routine he says, "My name is Mrs. Corrine Corfu." It doesn't set me on fire at this moment; however, to be fair, it is out of context and I'm not hearing Mel Brooks say it in his own inimitable fashion. In 1961, we howled.

Another gem:

Congratulations, your husband is a fag.
Love,
Lemmon

Of course, ever since *Some Like It Hot,* Jack Lemmon had been a close chum. Such a talent! I think we sent him a congratulatory greeting which went something like this: "Good luck. Be sure to let us choose the dress you wear when you pick up your Oscar."

Here's a riddle:

Dear Janet:
Bravo and hold thumbs.
Larry Olivier

I never figured this one out. It must have been an English saying—instead of crossing your fingers you hold your thumbs?

Such a nice surprising wire arrived:

Dear Miss Leigh:
Congratulations on your being nominated for an Academy Award. I thought you were just great. Hope you win.
Sincerely,
Larry Lincoln, Clerk
Western Union, Canon Drive
Beverly Hills

I guess he was delivering so many telegrams to the house he got caught up in the excitement. Beverly Hills was still pretty much a small town then, and everybody knew everybody. The shops, the grocers, the cleaners, the camera store, the five-and-dime (yes, there *was* still a five-and-dime), the fabric shop—it was a little community set in the middle of this huge metropolis.

I received hundreds of notes, wires, flowers, bottles of champagne. It's impossible to mention all of the thoughtful people I heard from. But I am going to jot down some names you will recognize, and I hope you're as impressed as I was (and still am): Anne and Kirk Douglas, Spencer Tracy, Greer Garson, Peter Falk, Rosemary Clooney and Jose Ferrer, Sammy Cahn, Jimmy Van Heusen, Irving "Swifty" Lazar, Audrey and Billy Wilder, Shirley Jones, Edith Head, Blake Edwards, Edie and Bill Goetz, Rosemarie and Bob Stack, Helen and Marty Rackin, Ray Stark, NBC's David Tebet, *Hollywood Reporter*'s Mike Connolly, Bunny and Johnny Green, Edie and Lew Wasserman, and, of course, my dearest mentor, Lillian Burns Sidney.

A legion of good wishes from family members, school pals, business associates, and fellow set workers were also welcomed with deep gratitude. Morgan Hudgins, the PR man on my first picture fifteen years before, wrote a lovely letter. I was so touched to be remembered by such a diverse array of friends. I was an extremely fortunate lady.

Adding to my happiness was the announcement that I had also been nominated for a Golden Globe in the same category. The Golden Globe is a prestigious award given by the Foreign Press Association.

At the group's formal dinner on March 16, 1961, my name was revealed as the winner. My cup runneth over! I was so nervous my feet turned to lead, my knees to jelly, my head to empty. I forgot to thank Mr. Hitchcock or Tony Perkins. Actually, I don't remember exactly what I did say. I was just thrilled to win and be so compensated for the work I loved.

Tony catches up with Janet to congratulate her on winning the Golden Globe for Psycho.

Charles "Chuck" Walters asked Danny Kaye, my husband Tony and me to do an updated rendition of *Triplets* (from the musical *Band Wagon*) on the Academy Awards show. I was happy to be absorbed in rehearsals, so I didn't have time to think about the awards themselves.

April 17, 1961, was endless. Rehearsals for *Triplets* and also for the presenters kept us at the theater all day. We even dressed there. One consolation—we didn't have to walk down that traditional long red carpet laid out at the entrance of the theater. (I know I would have stumbled or something. I'm such a klutz, especially when I'm keyed up.)

Finally, the show was under way. First, we presented an award and then we hurried to our assigned seats to await the verdicts. Joseph Hurley and Robert Clatworthy, for Art Direction (Black and White); George Milo, for Set Decoration; and John L.

Russell, for Cinematography (Black and White), had already been eliminated. It wasn't an encouraging trend.

As each name was read, the camera panned to the nominee. I tried to look relaxed and cool, but it just wasn't in me. I was obviously feeling the strain; people told me that my small face almost disappeared. When the envelope was opened, the words rang out: "And the winner is, Shirley Jones for *Elmer Gantry*."

An electric shock ran through my body, and then, weirdly, a flood of relief. The wondering was over. I didn't have time for much reflection just then, because after applauding Shirley and her acceptance speech, we were quickly escorted back through the maze of corridors to prepare for our number. Then I was onstage again, cavorting with Danny and Tony in the zany, athletic *Triplets*.

Judy Garland, in New York for her Carnegie Hall concerts, called me later that night, and said, "I couldn't believe I was watching someone who had just lost the Oscar."

When I was getting out of my costume and back into my finery, Billy Wilder was proclaimed Best Director for *The Apartment*. *Now* came the tears. I adored Billy Wilder, but I so wanted Hitchcock to have that gold statue for *Psycho*. This was his fifth nomination (*Rebecca* in 1940, *Lifeboat* in 1944, *Spellbound* in 1945—when again he lost to Wilder, for *The Lost Weekend*— *Rear Window* in 1954, and now *Psycho* in 1960) and the Oscar had eluded him once more!

Of course I was disappointed that I hadn't won. I would be a damned liar if I said otherwise. But the votes were cast fair and square. It just wasn't my turn. And I *had* been nominated by my peers. And I would always have that joy.

I would also carry with me forever the solace of true friendship. Almost as many notes came *after* I lost as when I'd been nominated. For that, I still felt like a winner.

THE
EFFECT

Most everyone has a *Psycho* story. People remember where they saw it first, with whom they saw it, their reactions at the time, and the effect the film had on them afterward. Some stories are funny, some are sad, some are tragic—but all are interesting. Why don't we start with my aftermath, then work our way through the experiences of some others close to the film, and then segue into those who had no connection to the movie itself other than having seen it.

SECTION 1: MY AFTERMATH

It's true that I don't take showers. If there is no other way to bathe, then I make sure all of the doors and windows in the house are locked, and I leave the bathroom door open and the shower curtain or stall door open so I have a perfect, clear view. I face the door no matter where the showerhead is. The room, I might add, gets very wet.

A funny coincidence: I went to the eleventh Telluride Film Festival, where I was tributed. Among the films shown was Psycho, of course. When they ushered me into the wonderful rustic motel and the room where I'd be staying—guess what? Right! There was only a shower.

Prior to Psycho I was a relatively normal bather, but after was a different story. It wasn't the shooting of the scene that caused the damage, it was seeing the film in its entirety later.

Once *Psycho* was an established, no-joke hit, Mr. Hitchcock said something to me that absolutely broke my heart.

"You know, ol' girl, we can never work together again."

Tears welled up, and I started to ask him what he meant and then I stopped. I understood the why before he continued.

"No matter what role you played or how well you did it, if I was the director, you would still be Marion Crane to the audience." He saw how depressed I was and, as only he could, he said, "Now, however, if someone else directed, and I played your leading man, that would be a different cup of tea."

I have already said this, but I'll say it again: That man was tops!

So, those were unhappy outcomes of *Psycho* for me. Another unsettling after effect was the weird mail that I began to receive. A few bizarre creatures even sent tapes, describing what they would like to do to Marion Crane. Tony (Curtis) and I weren't sure how to handle these; our fan mail had always been so loving before.

Director/producer Mervyn LeRoy and his beautiful wife Kitty were visiting one day and our secretary interrupted us, quite upset. Another grotesque letter had arrived. Since Mervyn had just finished making *The FBI Story,* I think he felt qualified to take charge of the situation. He yanked his handkerchief from his pocket, then placed it over his hand before delicately plucking the letter from our secretary. He read the missive, his face registering, on a scale of one to ten, a ten for horror. Carefully he wrapped the paper and envelope in the handkerchief and tucked it safely in his pocket.

"I will send this directly to the FBI, along with any others you have. This must be investigated."

We were so indebted to him for his help and advice; at last we knew what to do with these cranks. We didn't recognize the humor in the situation until it hit us later: Mervyn had been very cautious not to blemish the letter with his fingerprints, but had

One of my wonderful baths with Jamie Lee and Kelly.

overlooked the fact that our secretary had touched it, the deliveryman had touched it, no telling how many people at various post offices had touched it. . . We could only hope the culprit's prints had not been completely obscured.

I did receive a visit from a couple of gentlemen from the Bureau. They had located two of the offenders. Evidently these two were "regulars," and the agency had been aware of them for some time. But the FBI men warned me to keep the Bureau informed of any further correspondence of any kind, because no one could be sure when such threats were serious and presented a real danger, or when one of the harmless ones might suddenly go off the deep end.

That was just dandy! One piece of mail had come from the Chicago area, and I was due to make an appearance there in the near future. We exercised considerably more security than usual on that trip, I can assure you.

In November of 1993, I was sent a letter from the FBI regarding the Freedom of Information Act, asking if I would want my FBI file. I thought it would be intriguing research for this book, so I filled out the request form.

I sent a follow-up letter in February of 1994 asking if the agency's response could be expedited because I had a publishing deadline.

I should have known better. The reply came promptly to tell me the bad news. At the end of 1993, the total requests for files numbered over ten and a half thousand and would require the review of an estimated four and a half million pages. There are over two hundred employees assigned full-time to this project, but due to the large volume of files on hand, delays in excess of one year are not uncommon. As of this writing, I have not been given any more information. But I tried!

Oddly enough, I still get kooky mail and phone calls. That is why I am so fussy about protecting the privacy of my telephone number. It is such a pain to constantly change numbers; I always forget to tell someone who should have my number and then get annoyed when that someone doesn't call me back.

As recently as four months ago, I was forced to get a new number. There had been too many hang-ups. And then I would get, "Hello, is Norman there?" And dumb me would brightly say, "Oh, you must have the wrong number!" And the voice would lower and say, "This *is* the Bates Motel, isn't it?"

That's all I need to hear! Get me AT&T.

My birthday is on July 6, which makes my zodiac sign Cancer, its symbol being the crab. It just dawned on me as I was writing this book that maybe that is why water has figured prominently in my life as often as it has. And my husband, Bob Brandt, was born on July 7, and he has certainly had encounters with water. Once, he almost drowned in a whirlpool on the Colorado River, and another time he was buried in an avalanche of wet snow for twenty minutes.

When I was young I never learned to swim very well. We didn't have any money for lessons, and maybe twice in the summer Mom would take me to the local swimming pool known as the Plunge, and I would paddle around in the shallow end trying to imitate the other youngsters. So I grew up with little confidence in the water.

Several misadventures didn't enhance my attitude either. One Sunday in 1948, during the filming of *Little Women,* Elizabeth Taylor invited me to her house near Malibu for a beach party. Roddy McDowall, Peter Lawford, Van Johnson, June Allyson, Dick Powell, and other friends were there. Two guys and another gal and I went for a ride on one of those World War II rubber dinghies. (Don't ask what possessed me, because I don't know.)

We paddled about a mile out, where the guys dove overboard with their fins and masks to take a look at the bottom. When they surfaced, they threw something in the boat, something slimy and slithery. It was a baby octopus, complete with its saclike body and eight sucker-bearing tentacles. Yuk! At the same moment the dinghy started taking on water; it had sprung a leak. Needless to say, I freaked! I didn't want to go in the water, not only because of my lack of swimming skills and fear of drowning, but also because I figured mama octopus couldn't be too far away from baby. I'd read about how they wrapped those tentacles around their prey and then squeezed their victim to death.

We ladies frantically attempted to bail water with our hands, while the guys swam and pushed us toward the shore. I became more hysterical, and when we were close to the beach, I jumped out and splashed and screamed my way in. The waiting group wrapped us in blankets and poured brandy down our throats. Even then I couldn't stop shaking.

In Africa, where I shot most of the film *Safari* (1955, with

Victor Mature), the location site was established three hours inland from Nanjuki at the base of Mount Kenya, in Kenya. As my luck would have it, when we arrived at this forsaken (but oh so exciting) camp, the English woman the company had hired in Nairobi for my stand-in and stunt double told me she was three months pregnant. I had recently suffered a miscarriage, and the memory of my loss was still tender. So I made a deal with the producer: Unless it was something absolutely ridiculous, I would do the stunts, but they had to pay her (clearly she needed the money or she wouldn't have taken the job; she wasn't a professional stuntperson).

At one point, my character innocently takes a ride on the river alone to see the sights in a rubber dinghy (I should have known). The excursion naturally led to near disaster, with the peaceful river becoming rapids and leading to a mammoth fall. A real dummy (not this one) was to go over the long drop. The close-up was done under controlled conditions at a chosen "baby" waterfall. The security people and the crew and natives organized a human circle to catch me at the bottom. The camera was low, aimed upward to give the illusion of great height.

I paddled furiously, trying to maneuver in the swirling mass, and bingo, over and down I went. I struggled in the water, tossed around like a cork, and then was stopped by my masculine net. Everything went really well. Except—a nearly fatal slip—when I overturned, I inadvertently gagged and swallowed some water. Need I say more. In London, Sir Neil Hamilton Fairley, a specialist in tropical diseases, diagnosed bacterial dysentery. The bugger was gone, but had caused considerable damage, and he said I would likely always suffer from a sensitive abdomen. He was right!

Peculiarly, I have had water scenes in quite a few other films (none with such spectacular results as in *Psycho,* however). A few samplings:

- In *Pepe* I had a meeting with Cantinflas while taking a bubble bath in a huge sunken tub.
- *Perfect Furlough* found me falling in a wine vat and cleaning up in an antique freestanding French bathtub.
- When the Russian spy deliberately strayed into an American zone base in *Jet Pilot,* what was the first thing the poor girl did when brought before John Wayne for interrogation? Why, she took a shower, of course.
- My tipsy flapper was pushed into a cascading fountain by Jack Webb in *Pete Kelly's Blues.*
- Dean Martin, Jerry Lewis, and yours truly, three daffy characters, ended up submerged in a river for the finale in *Living It Up.*
- And the pathetic soul in *House on Green Apple Road* was discovered hiding in—a shower!

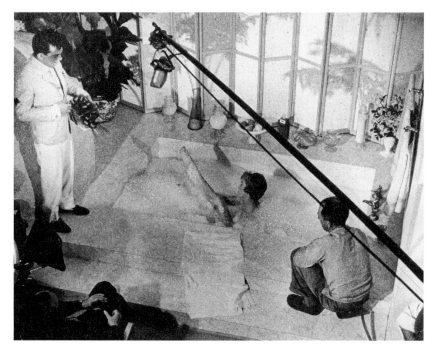

Janet and Cantinflas in Pepe.

In the tub again for The Perfect Furlough.

Come to think of it, motels haven't been too kind to me in films either. Besides the Bates Motel, there was that motel in *Touch of Evil* where Charlton Heston's bride was given a pretty rough time of it. But at least those terrifying experiences fared well in the annals of cinematic history.

Plainly, the lasting effect of *Psycho* for me is that I am writing this book thirty-five years later. I've made over fifty feature films and more than thirty television movies, as well as countless guest appearances, and even though I'm asked about other roles too, I am *always* asked about *Psycho*.

SECTION 2: ALFRED HITCHCOCK

No one really knows for sure the effect *Psycho* had on Alfred Hitchcock, because he never told anyone directly. In the myriad of publications about Hitchcock, the writers could only *surmise*

Janet, Dean Martin, and Jerry Lewis in Living It Up.

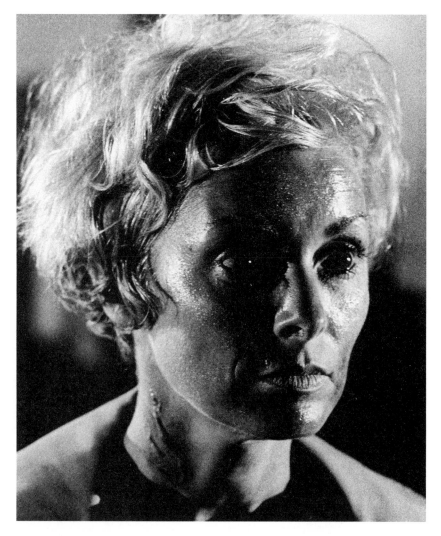

The pathetic shower rat in House on Green Apple Road.

the repercussions of "life after *Psycho.*" The information is all circumstantial: monetary returns, out-of-context quotes from interviews spread over years, personal opinions from colleagues, career moves, staff choices. But no one ever heard from his lips—unless it was the ears of his treasured wife Alma or his daughter Patricia—exactly how this particular film influenced his essence, his life.

And I know no more than others have found out. So I'm telling you up front, this is conjecture on my part. Still, some of these suppositions are reasonably safe to assume and I think they are accurate. Take the financial factor. *Psycho* was one of the largest-grossing black-and-white films in movie annals. Hitchcock sold his rights to *Psycho* and his television series to MCA in 1962, for 150,000 shares of MCA stock. He became a multimillionaire and the third-largest shareholder in Universal (MCA).

Certainly, he had to be proud of this achievement. He had braved new worlds, defied traditions—and won. But had he set a level of expectation for himself so high that even he couldn't reach it again? I don't know. I asked Joseph Stefano.

Joseph Stefano: "I know he was delighted with the success of Psycho. *But trying to top* Psycho? *I don't think that ever really*

At the motel in Touch of Evil.

entered his mind. Because in our discussions about Marnie *the subject never came up." [Stefano started working with Hitch on* Marnie, *which was supposed to be Hitchcock's next picture after* Psycho, *but it was postponed.]*

Maybe Stefano is correct. Hitchcock certainly kept challenging himself through his selection of material and his decision to create new stars. One associate felt that after *Psycho* he almost believed he had the Midas touch, that anything he touched would turn to gold.

Let's pursue that a bit. After *Marnie*'s first go-around was aborted, Hitchcock settled on *The Birds* as his next venture, with a completely inexperienced Tippi Hedren as his newest discovery. Hitchcock lost Stefano on this one.

Joseph Stefano: "I'm not crazy about birds, you know—stuffed is okay. Also, I had a funny feeling that we were starting from scratch. Because the short story that it was based on was short, but not a story."

The Birds proved to be a major undertaking; the special effects alone were a staggering obstacle. And, once again, it was an unconventional project.

Mr. Hitchcock ran a print of The Birds *for the Wassermans and Bob (Brandt, my husband) and me at Universal before all of the bird attacks were put in, and it was chilling even that way. But when I saw the final cut, with the full aerie assault, it was startling, to say the least.*

The picture furnished Hitchcock and Universal with much revenue, but it never reached *Psycho*'s monetary pinnacle. The critical acclaim was mixed, but there was nothing new about that. The public went, but they never embraced the movie as they had *Psycho*.

Robert Bloch [author of the novel Psycho*]: "It [The Birds] was not the film for which Hitchcock would be remembered."*

Marnie was released four years after *Psycho*. Stefano was asked to work on this one too, but had to decline again, because he was committed to producing the television show *Outer Limits*. Unfortunately, Stefano wasn't the only casualty on the film. The critics and public agreed—this one didn't work.

And no subsequent films attained the summit of *Psycho*. It

wasn't as if any of the pictures were poorly made, only that the ingredients never blended to their full potential.

I was making Harper *with Paul Newman when he signed to do* Torn Curtain *for Mr. Hitchcock. It co-starred Julie Andrews. I remember Paul remarking, "Hitchcock is going to rehearse for* two weeks *before* we start shooting."*
I thought to myself at the time, "Either this will end up being shot the way Hitch has already planned or it will be a complete disaster!"

Torn Curtain was a perfect example of the dilemma I was addressing. Here was a superior director and two megastars— enough talent to launch a rocket. But, for whatever reason or reasons, they just didn't come together.

Joseph Stefano: "I don't think he ever recovered from Psycho. But when we made it, Hitchcock was just trying to make a good movie. He seemed past the stage of needing to prove anything to anyone. I wish he'd called me and said, 'Let's do another picture for a million dollars.' It would have been a killer, but he never needed or wanted to do that kind of thing again."

Now you understand why no one knows for sure the effect of *Psycho* on Alfred Hitchcock.

SECTION 3: ANTHONY PERKINS

In our fact-finding interviews, a most interesting piece of information surfaced, something Anthony Perkins said to his oldest son, Osgood. It shouldn't really come as a surprise because it shows the integrity and depth of a truly gifted artist. But I would like to reveal his observation in the order of discovery.

I wish I'd had the foresight to talk with Tony about the effect of *Psycho* on him on one of the many occasions we shared time together after the movie was a success. But there was always such a variety of topics to discuss, it simply never entered my head. And when the thought finally did penetrate, it was too late.

We didn't have the kind of friendship where we had dinner every week or called each other every day. It was a very relaxed, comfortable comradeship. Whether we'd seen each other a week ago or six months ago, we picked up the beat as if it had been yesterday. He was so easy to be with, and so mentally provocative.

It has been said, and I think correctly so, that the true test of a friend's character is to travel with him or her. The best—or worst—will come out.

In the early sixties, probably 1962, Natalie Wood asked me to go to Buenos Aires, Argentina, to accept an award on her behalf. (I believe it was for *Splendor in the Grass*.) The internationally attended ceremony was Argentina's equivalent of the Oscars. The American representatives were David Miller, a respected director; Karl Malden, the talented actor; my husband Bob and I; and Anthony Perkins. The State Department used this as a goodwill cultural trip, and from Buenos Aires it sent us to Cuiaba, Brazil, for a similar function.

You have to understand a bit about my husband Bob. He is a very bright businessman, not too familiar with or unduly impressed by "showbiz," quite down-to-earth, very private, and extremely handsome. He did not previously know any of the participants on this jaunt. But it didn't take long; these were exceptionally congenial people. And he and Tony particularly hit it off.

Crowds, and crowd hysteria, unnerved Bob. I had toured South America for the United States Information Services in 1961, so I knew about the exuberance of the fans down there, but poor Bob was not prepared for this onslaught of humanity. When we stepped out of the limousine on the night of the festival, the police were hard-pressed to contain the mob behind the ropes.

Bob, and the officers, almost had apoplexy when I started to walk *toward* the masses of people gathered to see us.

I learned a long time ago that if a personality does NOT run away from people, you will not give them the excuse to surge forward to try to see you. When they realize you are really moving *to* them, the panic stops. It does work. And it did then. I just kept progressing slowly around the roped area, shaking hands, waving, and no one pushed. Of course, if you are too late and the frenzy has already erupted, then you need help to get the hell out of there.

The Russian contingent were a jovial bunch. And quite taken with my approach to public psychology (that is, when it was explained to them by their translator).

During the course of the trip Tony Perkins, Bob, and I passed the time with elaborate word games, including one in which one person would begin a limerick and then another would have to come up with the next line. As our journey continued, the verses became more and more risqué. Fortunately, no one around us spoke English, because we were often stuck on a stanza and the answer could come to us at any given moment. In Buenos Aires, the three of us went to a department store (I needed a washcloth, which our hotel had not provided, and I don't remember what the boys were looking for), and Tony had been stymied. The solution hit him when he was on the mezzanine. He leaned over the balcony and shouted down to us on the main floor the filthiest jingle yet. We could have been hauled in on obscenity charges. But it was fun.

We went to the airport on our way to Brazil with Tony and his driver, who was crazy—I swear the man was nutso wacko! He refused to have any vehicle in front of him, even if it meant crossing over to the oncoming lane. And a truck: "Get out of my way!"—no matter how big it was. He passed one bus and actually clipped it when he swerved back into his lane. I think the festival officials told the chauffeurs to get their celebrity passengers

The Russian contingent and the American representatives—Janet, Tony Perkins, David Miller, and Karl Malden—in Buenos Aires, Argentina, in the early sixties.

where they were going—pronto. I also think this one took his instructions too literally.

At the airport hundreds had gathered, waiting for us. This time I could not apply my theory, because they swarmed over the car before we could get out. It was a little scary—the car was rocked back and forth so hard we thought it might tip over. Fortunately police squads showed up before that happened and dispersed the throng. Never a dull moment!

In Cuiaba, the funniest incident of the trip occurred. We went to a television studio to tape a live show with one of Brazil's favorite interviewers. As usual, David, Karl, Tony, and I sat side by side in a sort of arc. Continuing the angle several chairs away, off camera, Bob lounged, waiting for us to finish. Each of us talked a bit with the nice lady, the camera moving down the line from one to the other.

When we had all spoken, she said, looking straight into the lens, "And now, my friends, what you have been waiting for. I am pleased to introduce Mr. George Maharis!" And the camera swung around—*to Bob!*

Bob watched in horror as the red light focused on him. He straightened up, completely flustered, not knowing what in the world to do. David, Karl, Tony, and I were at first confused and stunned. And then, when we realized her mistake, we were in convulsions. Tony doubled over and fell right on the floor. But we had to do all this quietly, because we couldn't embarrass the hostess by revealing her error to the audience.

She raved on, "Tell me, Mr. Maharis, how does it feel to know your series *Route 66* is the biggest thing in Brazil?"

Poor Bob! Out of the corner of his eye he could see us going bananas, but he bravely tried to carry on. "Fine!" His voice came out a high-pitched squeak. In all fairness to this woman, I did mention that Bob was very handsome; he had thick black hair and could have resembled George Maharis. Maybe she thought people looked slightly different in person.

The show finally ended, and we couldn't wait to get out of there so we could really explode. No need to tell you, I'm sure, this was the highlight of the entire tour—a tour that cemented Bob's and my relationship with Tony forevermore.

A much later encounter with Tony merits a mention. In 1982, Alexander Cohen produced the first television and stage spectacular "Night of a Hundred Stars" in New York. There was one segment about famous "couples." For instance: June Allyson and Van Johnson came out together, Dale Evans and Roy Rogers, Ginger Rogers and Fred Astaire, and so forth. Anthony Perkins and Janet Leigh were "the odd couple." Tony had been unable to attend the rehearsals (he might have been in the play *Romantic Comedy*). The other pairs had invented some "business" to do when they were introduced—a twirl or embrace or some identifying trademark.

When Tony finally appeared the night of the show, I said, "What should we do?" It didn't take him more than a minute to answer, "I'll escort you out very properly, we'll take hands and bow. Then we'll look at each other slowly, as if, wow, we couldn't believe the wild reception we just received, and then we'll humbly bow again in gratitude to the audience." It worked perfectly. But actually, we didn't have to completely make believe. The response *was* unexpectedly heartwarming.

Only now came a realization: Wouldn't it have been a thrill to have been directed by Anthony Perkins?

I spoke with Graziella, who was fan secretary to Tony and Berry. She had seen the movie a while back, before she was employed by them.

Graziella: "After I was hired, I would house-sit when they were out of town. I would think of Psycho *and always be frightened to be alone in their big, rather isolated house.*

"But there were no strange letters, no threatening ones. There were many, many letters, all loving the picture. But not blaming him as Norman. I thought he was proud of the picture."

Berry Perkins, Tony's widow, was kind enough to lend me some of Tony's clippings and stills. She told me that after our talks, and after I had called to see if by chance she had any candid shots, she had forced herself to go through Tony's office. I realized how painful that had to have been for her, and expressed my eternal gratitude. But she said she was glad, that I had been the catalyst that forced her to face a task she knew she would have to do sooner or later. I have such admiration for this lady.

In an interview given shortly after the picture opened, and which I'd never read, Tony had stated, "I was encouraged to remain in films because of *Psycho*'s success. Before, I actually had felt guilt-ridden. I thought maybe the movies just weren't for me."

And this was said after he had made (and in many cases been much acclaimed in): *The Actress, Friendly Persuasion, Fear Strikes Out, The Tin Star, Desire Under the Elms, This Angry Age, The Matchmaker, On the Beach,* and *Tall Story.*

In that same piece (written by Bob Thomas and appearing in the *New York World Telegram & Sun*'s feature magazine section on Saturday, January 14, 1961), Tony told Bob, "I believe I will be nominated, and Janet, too."

This was staggering knowledge. Until this very moment, I had never been aware that Tony had actually sought the nomination. I don't remember any ads, any deliberate campaign. I was, I am, devastated. Just completely undone. His disillusionment must have been deep.

We will never know if it was by chance or by design that Anthony Perkins spent the next few years, until 1965, making films in Europe. Was he so disappointed that he wanted out of Hollywood for a while? Or did these pictures just surface at this time?

One fact we know for sure: He was not immediately typecast after *Psycho*'s release. Following the eleven-week run of *Greenwillow* on Broadway, Tony accepted movies that allowed him to appear opposite some of the most talented and captivating leading ladies on the international film scene. And in roles that offered him a wide variety of challenges.

He was Ingrid Bergman's sensitive young lover in 1961's *Goodbye Again,* based on the novel by Françoise Sagan. Later that year, he was a troubled youth in love with his stepmother, played by Melina Mercouri, in *Phaedra.*

In 1962, he shared a mix of romance and mystery with Sophia Loren in *Five Miles to Midnight.* The following year he joined Jeanne Moreau in a multinational production of Kafka's

The Trial. A movie that was released in France in 1964, *A Ravishing Idiot*, teamed Tony with Brigitte Bardot.

When Anthony Perkins returned to the United States, he probably wasn't fully aware of the enormous impact of *Psycho,* and was definitely unsuspecting of any influence the film might have on his future roles.

It's true he was usually cast as an emotionally complicated character, but he only played a handful of off-kilter or downright deranged men in the three decades following his creation of Norman.

He gave stand-up performances in two films with Tuesday Weld that have become cult favorites, *Pretty Poison* in 1968 and *Play It as It Lays* four years later. He contributed marvelously to the ensemble casts of *Catch-22* in 1970 and *Murder on the Orient Express* in 1974. Other memorable Anthony Perkins performances can be seen in 1970's *WUSA* with Paul Newman and Joanne Woodward, in the 1978 television movie *First You Cry* opposite Mary Tyler Moore, and as the obsessed, sexually warped pursuer of Kathleen Turner in the controversial 1985 drama *Crimes of Passion.*

But he did come back to play Norman Bates in the three *Psycho* sequels in 1983, 1986, and 1990. And it was this fact, this reassociation with his most famous role, that has led to the impression that he seldom played anything *but* Norman-like characters.

Hilton Green produced *Psycho II* and *III* and *IV.* We were curious if anyone had had any trouble persuading Tony to be a part of the sequels.

Hilton Green: "Well, what happened with all of Tony's situations, he was very particular about the story and wanted to make sure that it was true to the character of Norman. I mean he was uncompromising about Norman's portrayal. Because as we all know, no one knew Norman better than Tony Perkins. And no one could love Norman better than Tony Perkins. And so after making certain that the character would stay consistent, he came aboard."

We also wondered if, while spending time with Hilton on the sequels, Tony had ever reflected on how *Psycho* had changed his life and career. Or if he had ever gone into any detail about being typecast as Norman—if that had been a problem.

Hilton Green: "We talked about that a couple of times. As I recall, he did accept that Psycho *was his most prominent role. He realized that it had made him visible as a big star. But I think it also hurt him, kept him from getting other parts. He had been a popular leading man, a very fine actor. It is something he will always be remembered for, but I still believe it prevented him from other roles."*

I posed the same question (about *Psycho*'s eventually having a negative effect on Tony's career) to Stefano.

Joseph Stefano: "I'm not sure about that. On one level, I agree. But on another—he had really been playing Bates. His way of dealing with the character was quite similar—you know, Fear Strikes Out, *it's his path to reaching a character. When Hitch told me that Tony Perkins was going to do* Psycho . . . *let me back up here. I had seen a run-through of* Look Homeward, Angel. *There was this big scene going on, and for the statue of the angel they had a clothes tree from backstage. They put it down and Tony was standing by this and we were to imagine that that was going to be the angel in the cemetery. The scene was being played and my eyes kept going to this young man standing there who had nothing to say throughout the whole scene. And I thought, he's taken the scene away from Jo Van Fleet and all the other people in it, and he's not saying a word.*

He was just standing there in such a way. I said, 'That's Norman Bates.' I mean not at the time, but later when I knew he was going to do Psycho. *My whole Norman Bates was based on Tony standing on stage."*

Again, we have conflicting observations about the positive and negative effects of *Psycho* on Anthony Perkins's professional life.

Tony Perkins may not have received any bizarre mail, but his wife had an experience after he died that topped any letter or tape I was ever sent. It was a situation so weird it was difficult to believe it actually took place, but it did. Both of her sons, as well as friends, witnessed it.

Apparently a person (whom I cannot identify, even by gender, for obvious reasons) arrived at Berry's home one rainy night (naturally, it had to be raining). The person explained the car they were driving had broken down and asked to use the telephone. Berry's heart of gold couldn't refuse, and she welcomed the person in, making coffee, urging the person to get warm by the fireplace. Needless to say, the repairman couldn't come out that night (possibly the person never called a real number). Sweet Berry offered the stranger shelter in her vacant garage apartment. Somehow or other, over a period of time, the person became ensconced in their lives, and they found themselves at the mercy of this yo-yo, who eventually ended up in Berry's kitchen threatening to commit suicide with a butcher knife.

Berry Perkins: "People used to say to me, 'Aren't you afraid to live in a house with a psycho like Norman Bates?' Or, 'Aren't you afraid to take a shower?'

"I was never afraid; it never occurred to me to even think about it. But when this incident happened, I became afraid. Because suddenly it was the image of the knife and the car; suddenly all that came rushing back to me."

When I first visited Berry, there wasn't a lock on the front gate. The next time I was there, she'd had a security system installed. What a sad commentary on our society today.

Berry Perkins: "I think it was totally unconscious. If anyone were to say to this person, 'Did your behavior have anything to do with Psycho?' *I doubt this person would recognize that and would believe the action came directly from other sources."*

Berry and Tony were married in August of 1973, quite a while after *Psycho*. The film had to have been discussed, though, and I was curious about the memories he shared with her regarding Hitchcock, and Tony's first viewing of the finished print.

Berry Perkins: "He loved Hitchcock. He said he had a great time with him, he was very respectful of him and thought he was a terrific man. And he adored you."[What else could she say? But it still made me very proud.]

"He talked more about you as a friend, not just about you in relation to the movie and work." [That made me even happier.]

"Tony never spoke to me about his reaction to seeing Psycho. *I would venture to say that he probably never saw it. He didn't like to see himself in films. Because when it was over, it was over. He never wanted to watch films of his."*

Berry and Tony's younger son, Elvis, was born in February of 1976. He was eighteen when I talked to him about his father and *Psycho*. I didn't know if he had even seen it.

Elvis Perkins: "Sure I saw it. I liked it, but I didn't think it was as scary as a lot of people had told me it was."

I questioned Elvis if his friends knew who his father was, and how they acted if they did.

Elvis Perkins: "I have the feeling that people who knew me would say to others, 'Oh, that's Anthony Perkins's son.'

"My friends would think that it would be scary to live in the same house with him or to take showers in the house.

"You know, I never thought about that before, not until that person came here."

Berry Perkins: "We did have an interesting experience when we first moved out here. A kid Elvis's age lived across the street, and our families used the same baby-sitter. For some reason, she thought it was funny Tony lived so close. Both children were about five or six. Psycho *came on television one night, and the baby-sitter made this poor young child sit and watch this movie. 'Because your neighbor is in this picture and you have to see it.' We carpooled, and very often Tony used to drive them to school. And for about six months after that, every time the child saw Tony, he would cry. His mother didn't understand what was happening, because she didn't know he had seen the movie. So the mother had to do all the carpooling after that, because the boy refused to get in the car with Tony."*

There is no equivocation in Berry's mind about the effect of *Psycho* on her husband's future work.

Berry Perkins: "Definitely it influenced his options. It was like he had a whole other life before Psycho, *a whole other career.*

"He voiced it to me privately, but he didn't even do that a lot. He was never much for sour grapes, you know what I mean? He didn't want to talk about things in a negative way. Because he was always very grateful that he was getting jobs; he was into a being-grateful-for-what-he-got kind of thing.

"But you could tell. You know—these monster parts came in all the time, as opposed to things which I'm sure he would have loved to do. We'd go to the movies and I couldn't help saying, 'God, you would have been so great in that part!' I tried not to say it too often, but it was so frustrating. All the Anthony Hopkins roles, all those kinds of things, but people just didn't think of him for those parts. I think he settled for less than he should have. I think that maybe if he had expressed his opinion more he might have been offered a variety of roles. I believe it's very hard

*to break out of a mold, and I can't think of anybody else who
had been that typecast. Not that severely."*

*I mentioned to Berry how Hitch had told me we could never
work together again because no one would be able to disassoci-
ate me from Marion Crane and* Psycho *and Hitchcock, and how
maybe that type of industry mentality did the same number on
Norman Bates and Anthony Perkins.*

The oldest Perkins son, Osgood, went to the University Of
Southern California film school for one year and then trans-
ferred to an eastern college, where he continued in the same
major. I was eager to hear if *Psycho* was utilized in some part of
the courses.

*Osgood Perkins: "I wasn't exactly surprised by this fact,
but it certainly was a little startling that* Psycho *was such a cor-
nerstone of what all the film school teachers were talking
about. I mean, it seemed to me that* Psycho *was brought up in
every class that I was ever in, and it was in most of the textbooks. At USC, there was a class just on Hitchcock, which
included* Psycho, *of course.*

*"The shower scene is in a lot of textbooks, outlined shot by
shot, all seventy-two angles, or however many there were. They
devote whole chapters to it. They talk about the use of cameras,
they talk about dissolves, they talk about performances, they talk
about all that. And it's always brought up by the professor as
The Example.*

"I took one subject called Horrors, Science Fiction, and
Fantasy. *And they brought up* Psycho *as the turning point in
1960, along with a movie called* Peeping Tom, *for the horror
persona—in that before monster movies were being made in
which 'the horror' was something outside of mankind, like a
robot from outer space, or the creature from the black lagoon.*

Horror had nothing to do with people, it had only to do with things outside the human being.

"But the horror personality which took over in the sixties turned out to be horror from WITHIN, *horror from within the man.* Psycho, *is very much about Norman's inner torment; not that he's a monster on the outside, he's a monster on the* INSIDE.*"*

I was so impressed with this young man that I began to calculate . . . let's see, he was born in 1974, my granddaughter was born in 1986—is twelve years too big a difference in ages?

Before asking Osgood the big Q, I wanted to find out a little more about him and the family relationship.

Janet: "Because your Dad knew you were leaning toward the film industry, did he discuss movies in general or Hitchcock in particular?"

Osgood Perkins: "He was more inclined to sort of let me figure things out for myself. I appreciated that. He wasn't going to guide me and tell me what he thought about everything, and therefore not let me form my own opinions. Once I decided to go to film school, he gave me my own space and said, 'You go figure it out for yourself.' Which is invaluable advice in parental conditioning."

I had to offer my own opinion here because the situation we were discussing was so parallel to that of mine with my girls, Kelly and Jamie.

Janet: "We shouldn't say what our perceptions are, or what happened to us, because the time span is too wide."

Osgood Perkins: "Exactly! Everything is different. Every situation is different.

"This house was never about the movies. My relationship with my father, my brother's relationship with my father, my mother's relationship with my father, was never about the movies, not for a second. This house was about our family.

"Even though our lifestyle and the fact that we are comfortable in our life has a lot to do with Psycho—*I mean, we have to attribute a lot of our life to that movie, for sure. But we never sat around and talked about it all the time. You know, it's a job. I don't think very many dentists come home and talk to their wife and kids about their day at the office. 'Gee, honey, I did this great cavity today.'"*

I liked him more and more. He was so rational and sensible. Osgood gave the definitive answer regarding the effect of Psycho *on the life of his father.*

Osgood Perkins: "I asked Dad once, 'If you could go back to 1959 and either take or not take the role in Psycho, *knowing that taking it would mean that you would be typecast for the rest of your life, what would you do?'*

"He thought about that for a while. It seems to me that he might have thought about it for a whole day. And he came back and said, 'I would definitely take it!'

"I think it was because he understood about the integrity of the part, and not the integrity of one's career as a whole. He was more interested in doing right by one part than in doing right by one's entire career. Instead of spreading himself thin over a bunch of movies, he would rather have made an impact in one picture, which he did."

Janet: "Richard Burton once said that an actor is lucky if he is remembered for even one great role. For your father, Norman Bates was such a role. He was just so brilliant as Norman that the industry would not allow him to be anyone else."

Osgood Perkins: "Exactly. And I think a lot of people who cast him after Psycho *missed the richness of what he had done. Because he really gave a dual performance that was very deep. When I see* Psycho *with friends of mine now who have never seen it, the immediate reaction that they have to Norman in the first half hour to forty-five minutes is sympathy—nothing else. When they put my father in those mediocre horror roles after that movie, they failed to understand the depth of what he had done—Dad was far beyond those other parts.*

"Because never for a minute in Psycho *do you not feel bad for the poor guy. In the end, you find yourself saying, 'Well, gee, I was kind of siding with him the whole time.' Even when he was arrested. And to implicate the audience as feeling sorry for the killer . . . I mean you felt guilty, because you had sympathized with a murderer. That was one of the best things I think he did in that movie. And every time I see* Psycho, *it astonishes me that you feel not as much scared of him as you do sorry for the torment that is going on inside his mind.*

"What was equally unpleasant about the fact that he was typecast for so long was—he was mis-*typecast. It wasn't even that he was typecast into the compassionate parts that he liked to play and that he was good at playing; he was typecast into very straight villains or very straight madmen who didn't have the layers of a Norman. Roles of murderers, roles of insane people— that isn't what* Psycho *was all about and that isn't what Norman Bates was all about. People plainly overlooked the fact that he was a fine actor, not just a portrayer of psychopaths."*

Now we know. And now we know more about the quality of the man and actor Anthony Perkins. I'm sure he always knew what manner of men his sons were, but I have to tell you my feelings. He would be so proud of them—how they think, how they have grown mentally and spiritually. He and Berry did a heck of a job.

SECTION 4: WHAT A CAST

Vera Miles, John Gavin, Martin Balsam, John McIntire, Simon Oakland, Vaughn Taylor, Frank Albertson, Lurene Tuttle, Pat Hitchcock, John Anderson, and Mort Mills. What a stellar cast Mr. Hitchcock had assembled. Each actor was so right on. Everyone stood out, whether he or she was in one scene or throughout the entire film.

The personal reviews were excellent. And the striking success of the movie itself must have been music to the ears of agents lucky enough to represent these talented thespians.

I believe the enduring legacy of their performances is in the memorable images we the audience carry with us whenever we think of *Psycho*:

• Vera Miles, turning Mother to face her and hitting the light-bulb. (It has been documented in many articles how movie-goers screamed out to the screen, "Stay away from that house, Lila!" Or, "Don't go down to the cellar.")

• John Gavin, bare-chested, looking down at Marion on the bed. Sam struggling with Mother, only to reveal Norman.

• Martin Balsam, bantering with Norman in that marvelous scene in the motel office. Arbogast's shocking murder.

• John McIntire—his expression when Sam and Lila tell Sheriff Chambers that Arbogast saw Norman's mother.

• Simon Oakland, astonishing us all with Dr. Richmond's explanation of Norman and Mother at the end.

• Vaughn Taylor—the bewildered look Mr. Lowery gives his employee Marion when he sees her driving out of town.

• Frank Albertson—so beautifully rotten when Cassidy dangles money in front of Marion's face.

• Lurene Tuttle, delightfully suggesting that Mrs. Chambers's Sunday dinner would be the cure-all for the troubled Sam and Lila.

• Pat Hitchcock, noting that the rich oilman probably noticed

Caroline's wedding ring and therefore flirted with Marion instead of her.

- John Anderson, wondering how a buyer could outpressure "California Charlie" the car salesman.
- Mort Mills, wearing the menacing mirrored dark glasses of the highway patrolman.

SECTION 5: JOSEPH STEFANO

The repercussions from *Psycho* are still reverberating for Joseph Stefano. He gives seminars all over the country about movies and writing, and he said *Psycho* ends up the usual focal point.

Joseph Stefano: "It's fascinating to see people's reaction when you discuss someone or something and contradict their preconceived concept. For instance, I talk about Hitchcock at these seminars, and I tell them about our relationship, how open to suggestion he was. And how some days we didn't feel like talking about Psycho, *so I would ask if I could run* Shadow of a Doubt? *Or* Rebecca? *Or something! And he would say, 'Sure, set it up.'*

Then I would return and spend three hours asking questions. Why did you do this and why did you do that and how did this come about and what made you take this level on things instead of that one? He would sit for hours. And it always blows their minds, because this is not how people see Hitchcock.

"This happened to me after the first time a group of friends saw Psycho *with my wife and me. When we came back to the house, my friends were giving me cryptic side glances, because they couldn't believe that this is what I had been writing all these months. Funny thing—they seemed to believe that in order to write this movie, I had to be a little like the character we had been watching in the theater.*

"I guess that happens often with actors, too. Like if you

don't have some of that in you, you couldn't possibly play that part. But it is very much the thinking toward writers."

Janet: "It is the same with actors, trust me. People forget we get paid to convince them we are a certain character. That's our job. Just like yours is to write believably.

"Now I must ask you—this was supposedly something you said in another book: 'Psycho was the worst career mistake I ever made!'"

Joseph Stefano: "How could I have said that? Obviously my intent was misconstrued. As I recall, we were discussing the time when I had started preparing Marnie, *the first go-around with the picture, when Grace Kelly was reportedly doing the film. And I was very excited, as it was to be a real Hitchcock movie, with the return of his famous leading lady. I didn't mean my enthusiasm to be a put-down of* Psycho!"

Something Stefano had touched on briefly returned as a question. When he and I had discussed how Tony had been typecast, he said in passing that so had he. How so?

Joseph Stefano: "I did feel the offers I received for quite some time were limited in scope to the genre of Psycho. *Fortunately, that identification wasn't as long-lasting as Tony's."*

I also discovered that Stefano's attitude was similar to Tony's regarding the typecasting he had to endure. He, too, would rather have done one script exceptionally well, whatever the consequences.

It was time to approach the topic of *Psycho IV*, which Stefano also wrote. And which was my own personal favorite of the sequels. And which was certainly an "effect" of the original *Psycho* on Stefano.

Joseph Stefano: "The people at Universal called me and said they wanted me to do it. I said I would be interested if it were a prequel rather than a sequel.

· *"I went to talk to them. There were eight people sitting in the room. I said, 'We open on* The Oprah Winfrey Show *and her subject is "Those Who Killed Their Mother." Somebody phones in and it is Norman.'*

"They all just sat there—mouths opened in wonder. Of course we couldn't use Oprah Winfrey, it was just an example. They were flabbergasted. Then they said, 'Almost any direction you take is going to work. Would you go and tell Tony [Perkins] what you just told us?'

"So I said sure and went to his house. By this time, three days later, I had worked out the whole outline, how Norman was really coming around—that he was married, happy, having sex with his wife, which he had never been able to do before. And then something happens which sets him off toward the end of the movie.

"He loved it. He grinned that Tony Perkins grin of his and said, 'You're making me stretch in this, aren't you?' I said, 'True, Tony. I don't want to see the Norman Bates that I have seen now for three pictures. Norman is past that. He has had all this fierce therapy and all this stuff is going on. His life has changed; he loves this woman.'

"And Tony did it. He really grabbed you in that movie. He loved the fact that this was a different Norman. And he had approval. I mean, if he hadn't bought my idea, we wouldn't have done the movie.

"And I liked showing the mother, seeing her, seeing who this woman was!"

SECTION 6: HILTON GREEN

We've already established *Psycho*'s effect on Hilton Green: He went from first assistant director on *Psycho* to producer on *Psycho II*, *Psycho III* and *Psycho IV*. And now he's a producer at Price Entertainment.

SECTION 7: BERNARD HERRMANN

Mr. Herrmann's endowment from *Psycho* will benefit not only film buffs, but music lovers for generations.

It is well known that Mr. Hitchcock had not wanted music written for the shower sequence; in actuality he hadn't wanted it for any of the scenes at the motel. It is also familiar territory that Bernard Herrmann and Alfred Hitchcock collaborated on several projects before and after *Psycho,* and that Herrmann was secure enough and crotchety enough to match wills or cross swords with Hitchcock at any given time.

A happy reunion of Tony, Janet, and Hilton Green on the Florida set of Psycho IV: The Beginning.

Peggy Robertson: "There was a similar situation on North by Northwest. *Hitch didn't want any music behind the scene where Cary Grant is chased by the crop-dusting plane. But Benny [as Herrmann was called by close associates] took it upon himself to compose a theme for it. Ultimately, however, Hitch decided against using it."*

Herrmann had a revolutionary idea for the scoring of *Psycho*—to use only strings. He then proceeded to implement his concept, and included the motel and shower scenes without Hitchcock's permission. Of course, the result is history.

Peggy Robertson: "Even with his prickly personality, Benny was not above accepting constructive criticism, especially from someone he respected as much as Hitch. We had the first run-through of the picture with Benny's scoring, and near the end, down in the cellar, Hitch listened to what Benny had written. Hitch said, 'Well, Benny, it's great, but you missed a terrific point!'

"And Benny in a huffy tone shouted, 'What? What?' Hitch explained, 'You should repeat that marvelous string theme from the shower scene. As Tony comes rushing down the cellar stairs, you should hear that theme again.'

"Benny thought for a minute and said quietly, 'That's a good idea.'

This typified the nature of their relationship—and in this instance, Hitch nearly doubled Herrmann's salary.

Herrmann created masterpieces that encapsulated Hitchcock's works—the highs and lows, the blacks and whites of our souls.

Joseph Stefano: "Hitch was taken with the screaming violins."

Robert Bloch: "It was quite innovative, discordant—not the sort of thing one usually expected with that kind of motion pic-

*ture. It threw me for a loop. I was not quite prepared for such . . .
screeching."*

I was in Seattle from April 27, 1994 to May 1, 1994. I had
been asked to promote and appear at a concert of the Northwest
Chamber Orchestra. The theme of the evening was "From Hol-
lywood to Seattle," and the program included Aaron Copland's
Music for the Theater, Sir William Walton's *Sonata for String
Orchestra,* Antonio Vivaldi's *Guitar Concerto in D, and* Bernard
Herrmann's *Psycho—A Narrative for Orchestra.* Obviously, the
latter was the reason for my invitation.

I had never heard the score separately before, so prior to the
performance at Kane Hall on the University of Washington campus, Wendy Williamson, the PR person for the orchestra, played
a tape for me as we were driving back to the hotel. The sky had
turned dark while we were inside for our last interview, and it
had started to rain. We were so engrossed in the music, which
evoked the film's visuals, and so enveloped by Seattle's ominous
clouds that when the strings went "whang, whang, whang," we
damn near jumped out of the car.

The orchestra, conducted by Adam Stern, was electrifying. I
couldn't get over the power, the emotion of that piece. All of the
selections were excellent and very moving, but naturally, *Psycho*
was the most potent for me.

In the 1970s, Bernard Herrmann conducted the London
Philharmonic Orchestra in a shortened translation of *Psycho*'s
music. That decade, he also led the National Philharmonic
Orchestra in a recording of the entire score.

I met Bernard Herrmann's widow in October of 1994. We
each had been asked to attend a Hitchcock tribute in Omaha,
where they showed *Psycho* and *North by Northwest*—both of
which, of course, had been scored by her husband. The evening
benefited the Nebraska AIDS Project, and it was an extremely
successful affair.

Lucy Herrmann is a wonderfully vibrant, eloquent, charming woman. I wish I had known Bernard Herrmann better; I have a feeling, since encountering his wife, that we would have all been good friends.

Mrs. Herrmann confided that Bernard had often deplored the lack of recognition given to movie scores by people, including actors. She added that it would have warmed his heart to hear my comments about the tremendous contribution his music had made to *Psycho.*

I explained to her that in my opinion, except for the special circumstances of a *Psycho,* not singling out a music score is actually a tribute to the composer. It means that the background music melded so perfectly into the dramatic intent that the audience never separated the different elements. And that, I believe, is the supreme compliment.

I have discovered and rediscovered so much in the process of writing this book, I am absolutely delighted I decided to do it.

Section 8: Robert Bloch

The New York Times, obituaries section, Sunday, September 25, 1994. Robert Bloch, Author of *Psycho* and Many Such Tales, Dies at 77.

"Robert Bloch, the prolific mystery writer whose novel *Psycho* was adapted for the classic Alfred Hitchcock horror film, died on Friday at his home in Los Angeles. He was 77. . . ."

"Mr. Bloch had joked to friends that his obituary would begin with *Psycho,* a novel that was just a tiny part of his flood of work. . . ."

"Ray Bradbury said the 1960 film of *Psycho* marked '. . . the beginning of a dark period when we made films based on psychotic reality rather than mythological things. . . . Suddenly we were confronted with the fact that our showers were not safe.'"

"The author Harlan Ellison said, 'Mr. Bloch was surely on

a level with Poe. . . . He set the tone for the modern dark fantasy . . . one of the first authors to examine the motivations and minds of serial killers . . .'"

"Mr. Bloch himself was described by Mr. Ellison as 'the kindest, gentlest human being who ever lived.' Mr. Ellison speculated that Mr. Bloch's interest in the criminal mind had arisen from his own open and honest personality. 'These characters were so utterly alien to him.'"

There are many of us who are very grateful to Robert Bloch, for his talent and creativity, and for launching a project named *Psycho*.

SECTION 9: THE PUBLIC

This section is going to be riveting, because it involves the effect of *Psycho* on you—your reactions, your experiences, your memories.

- Diane Walker is a *Time* magazine photographer, assigned mostly to the White House and the president, which makes her a world traveler and an extremely intelligent, informed lady; she's also an attractive, endearing, cherished friend. We were at a dinner party recently and I was discussing this book with a *New York Times* correspondent. Diane entered into the conversation. "Oh, I couldn't take a shower or go into a motel without seeing you in that movie. I'll never forget the blood pouring out and the knife going into your body. Oooh!" She was dumbfounded when I explained she couldn't possibly have seen that—it wasn't in the picture. The only blood was at the end, going down the drain. Her imagination had created those images—provoked, of course, by Mr. Hitchcock.

  And this is a very sophisticated woman.

- William from Massachusetts wrote, "I saw *Psycho* when I was fourteen years old in Washington, D.C. I vividly remember being literally shocked and unimaginably surprised by the brutality of the shower scene. The effects lasted long after I left the theater; in fact, I never forgot the feelings. I also recall the other patrons walking out with disbelief etched on their faces. I've watched it since, of course, and it always has that impact."

- Pam from Los Angeles: "When I heard about the book you were writing, it brought back memories. I was six months pregnant with my son when I went to see *Psycho*. When the murder in the shower began, I started to hyperventilate, and I rushed out to the lobby, as I was afraid I might go into false labor or something. After a while I felt better, but I didn't go back to see the rest of the picture—although I have since, and loved it! The funny thing is, my son Tim, who is now thirty-four, has never been able to watch scary movies of any kind. Is it possible *Psycho* frightened him prenatally?!"

- While I was in Seattle for that Northwest Chamber Orchestra concert, I was thoroughly covered by all the media—radio, television, and print. I was going up in the hotel elevator around the third day, along with a couple. The three of us exited on the same floor, and it turned out they were right across the hall from my suite. That prompted them to ask if I had heard the ruckus early that morning. I explained I was so tired I wouldn't have heard an elephant walking in my room. Evidently, about 5:00 A.M., they'd been awakened by a pounding noise. The man looked out the peephole, and there was a guy in his undershorts beating at my door. My neighbor rattled his doorknob and the fellow took off, with the newspaper that had been lying at my door clutched in his hot little hand. My picture was on the front page, I found out later, when I received another copy of the newspaper.

   A little scary, right?

- In Seattle on the night of the performance, conductor Adam Stern and I spoke for about an hour before the music started— I gave a few remarks, and then had a question-and-answer session with the audience. Naturally, I mentioned I was doing research for this book. During the intermission a gentleman named Alan introduced himself and told me his two *Psycho* stories. When Alan first saw the film, he was stationed at El Toro marine base in California. The showers were separate from the sleeping quarters, rather isolated, and not well lit. After seeing *Psycho,* these big, burly, tough marines, who had been accustomed to showering before bed, backed off. "I don't think I need a shower tonight, I'll just wait till tomorrow," one mumbled, looking over his shoulder. The others agreed.

Alan's girlfriend had never seen *Psycho,* so when it was shown on television in Seattle fairly recently (in preparation for the concert, I would assume), the two of them settled down to watch it. The lady was very frightened, very nervous. She was screaming and holding on for dear life (I have a hunch he didn't mind that part). Just as she had begun to calm down, before Arbogast's demise, a commercial interrupted. They were advertising steak knives with close-ups of the knives, the blades, the sharpness of the edges. And the lady completely freaked out again. Strange coincidence or clever programming?

I also thought I'd share with you a few brief examples of letters I have received recently:

- Billy: "*Psycho* is still one of my favorite movies. Its place in cinema history is assured, along with your wonderful performance. I am also eagerly awaiting the book you and Christopher Nickens are preparing about the cultural phenomenon known as *Psycho.*"
- Fred of Indiana: "I am writing because I have just read where you are working on a book about *Psycho* and I want to tell you how much I am looking forward to reading it. . . . Even though I am only twenty-five, I have always enjoyed films from the fifties and sixties."
- Mary Ann Fortuna (in the Legal Department at Universal Stu-

dios) had her own *Psycho* story to tell me. "Oh, I know just where I was when I saw *Psycho* first. I was about thirteen years old, and I was baby-sitting our neighbors' two St. Bernard puppies. They never liked to leave them alone—afraid of dognapping. So I curled up with the two dogs on my lap. And as the movie progressed, I became more and more frightened. I hugged the doggies so hard; I couldn't let them go. I was too fearful to move, to get up and turn the television off, to do anything. I just clutched the pups and prayed for safety."

- For reasons I'm sure you will readily understand, there will be no names or locations referred to in this next offering. My thanks to the sender; your contribution was gratefully received.

"On the *Vicki!* show you mentioned that you were doing a book concerning the movie *Psycho* and how it affected people who had seen it. As for me, showering became a frightening task and I was very fearful; but, for a friend of mine, 'Mr. X,' it had a far-reaching effect. I'm now sixty-three years old and I still remember this story. 'X' and I went to _____ Junior High School and then _____ High School. 'X' was rather a strange fellow—not too many friends and very cruel to animals.

"He was raised by his grandmother in _____. To the best of my recollection the story went something like this. One evening, the aunt of 'X' was found stabbed to death and stuffed under the bed. Since many clues were left in the apartment, 'X' was a prime suspect. The police were looking for him and his automobile; they spotted him on _____ Street. He had just picked up a lady who was waiting for a bus on _____ Avenue. The police stopped him and questioned him. Luckily the police interfered, otherwise this could have been his second victim.

"In the trial, it came out that on that day, 'X' had seen the movie *Psycho,* and that was the triggering force behind the murder of his aunt. 'X' was convicted of the crime and put to death. Ironically, 'X' was mentally ill and if the crime had happened today, he would be put into a mental hospital. Although the story is sad, but true, I think it might be interesting to the readers of your book."

And alas, this deplorable tale, I have been told, was not the only such account. What concerns me today is—if such harmful reactions could be produced by *Psycho*, where you didn't actually see weapon penetration or blood gushing or nudity—what repercussions are there today, when you see bullets tearing into bodies, knives practically disemboweling victims, complete sexual acts?

It's an old dilemma! Do we put the tail or the head first? Should the public tell film and television producers that we won't go to see excessive violence and that we'll boycott those offerings in which it occurs? Or should the producers, on their own, say we won't give the audience so much graphic sex and violence? The problem is at a stalemate: The people still flock to theaters or tune their sets in to the shockers, and the producers argue that they are in the business of providing the public with profitable entertainment. 'Tis a predicament!

Of course, *Psycho*'s ongoing impact manifests itself in a variety of ways. There are the theme parks at Universal Studios in Hollywood and a newer one located in Orlando, Florida. On the Hollywood Universal tour, one can see the *Psycho* house and the Bates Motel. And in Orlando there is a Hitchcock Pavilion, and included in it is a "skit" on the shower scene from *Psycho*.

I attended the official opening of the pavilion in Orlando. It was a wonderful three days. Tony Perkins was shooting Psycho IV *at that time and I was able to visit with him and Hilton Green on the sets. There were many stars present for those three days, among them Michael J. Fox, Charlton Heston, Jimmy Stewart, Robert Wagner, Jill St. John, and countless others. Tony and I put a piece of a shower curtain in a time capsule for the opening day ceremonies. When it's opened many, many years from now, I wonder if anyone will still remember* Psycho. *Then again, it has survived thirty-five years already.*

SECTION 10: A PSYCHO POTPOURRI

Hitchcock stories are a legend of their own. These have appeared before in print, but I have to tickle your fancy with a few, just in case you missed them.

- This is a radio spot Hitchcock made after the release of *Psycho*: "Ever since I made *Psycho,* the bottom has dropped out of the bathtub industry. So bathe now, before you see the film, or you may never bathe again."

- On Johnny Carson's *Tonight Show,* Hitchcock told of a letter he had received: "This man had a problem. You see, the man's wife saw the French film *Diabolique* [in which a corpse supposedly rises out of the water in a bathtub, very much alive, and the wife in the picture literally dies of fright]. And the man's wife wouldn't take a bath after that. Then his wife saw *Psycho* and refused to take a shower. Now what is he to do, as she is getting difficult to live with? I immediately told him, 'Send her to the dry cleaners.'"

- This has nothing to do with *Psycho,* but it is one of my favorites. Hitchcock was shooting a film and the producer had "suggested" to Hitchcock that he use the producer's "friend" for a small role. The girl was desperately trying to be noticed by the famed director. One day she pulled up a chair, sat down, leaned over conspiratorially, and asked, "Mr. Hitchcock, which do you think is my best side?" He answered, "You're sitting on it!"

Mr. Hitchcock, surprisingly, answered the tons of mail he received, very patiently and meticulously.

- A New Zealand fan wrote and asked if she could visit his set when she was on holiday in Los Angeles. The letter was sent in January 1959, and almost a year later, he allowed her onto the *Psycho* set.

Unfortunately, I was not working while she was there. It would have been interesting to meet her, and to observe how he reacted to her. It's unusual for directors to be that indulgent. And Hitchcock was quite shy, which is one reason he preferred to work with people he knew.

- A fan from New York spotted a faux pas: The highway patrolman checked Marion's driver's license against her license plate. The person pointed out he would have needed the registration to check the plate. Hitchcock replied that in his experience, when a cop stopped a car he looked it all over, regardless of whether he was checking anything out or not.
- Another claimed the bed had too deep an imprint for a lightweight skeleton when Vera examined Mother's room.
- Several people thought that the close-up of Marion's eye was a cheat, that it was a still.
- One female high school student requested a copy of Simon Oakland's speech at the conclusion of the film to help educate herself about mental illness.
- A clever would-be sleuth wrote, "Marion's license plate should have been '59 instead of '56." Hitchcock explained,

MOTHER GOOSE AND GRIMM

AND NOW, NORMAN'S MOTHER, MRS. BATES, WILL CUT THE CAKE...

THE FAMOUS 'BABY SHOWER' SCENE FROM PSYCHO.

"All California cars, at that time, had '56 plates, but they applied new stickers each year to update them."

- A couple of people caught the fact that, medically, Marion's eyes should have been dilated after death.

Sorry about that! I couldn't quite manage it. And I don't think even Hitch would have expected me to make the supreme sacrifice just to be medically correct.

- A British woman complained that after seeing the film, she and her mother couldn't take a flat they were considering because the bathrooms were similar to the one in the film.
- A man from Batesville, Indiana, asked if he could buy the Model A Ford that Vera walked by in the Bates Motel parking lot.
- One irate moviegoer wrote in to say she would go to the local library if she felt the need to learn anything about abnormal psychology.
- An offended music lover was livid: "Because Norman had a recording of Beethoven's *Eroica,* did that indicate that listeners of the symphony were deranged?"

It's astonishing to me that viewers would notice such small details and react to them. I was not aware of any of these things and I was *in* the movie.

Psycho's ongoing popularity is evidenced by the persistent requests to use portions of the picture or something connected with the film for mercantile purposes. For example, Universal agreed to loan Hard Rock Orlando, a nightclub, the "*Psycho* Knife." It remained the property of Universal, but Hard Rock Orlando was allowed to display it in rooms designated for film memorabilia.

Universal has received a quantity of letters over the years asking permission (which it has denied) to adapt the story of *Psy-*

Lincoln Center Film Society honoree Alfred Hitchcock flanked by Janet and Princess Grace of Monaco.

cho for stage musicals. They've received more than five requests in the last four years. Sounds weird. Were they thinking *Phantom of the Opera* here?

Radio and television commercials have imitated the music and the shower scene from *Psycho* for ages. There was a comic book version of the movie. Copycat movies have appeared, and comedians have had a field day with the material.

Mel Brooks did a hilarious burlesque of the shower scene in his Hitchcock spoof, *High Anxiety.*

A friend from Las Vegas, Barbara Nosek, after hearing about this book, sent me a cartoon and print of one of the attractions at the new Planet Hollywood nightclub in Las Vegas. She also made a funny comment. "I wonder if that movie had an unintentional environmental message, in the form of water conservation—anyone who ever saw it surely began taking much shorter showers."

My last mention is from the delightful film *Four Weddings and a Funeral*. Hugh Grant attends the Scottish wedding of his true love, Andie MacDowell. While there, he runs into an ex-girlfriend, who attempts to rekindle their earlier relationship.

"Did I behave atrociously last time?" she coyly asks.

He replies, "Remember the shower scene in *Psycho*?"

She nods.

"Scarier!" is his retort.

As has been said by people far wiser than I, "Imitation is the sincerest form of flattery."

EPILOGUE

Sculptress Camille Nathanson recalls an evening of entertainment in the fall of 1960 vividly: "I was living in Greenwich Village at the time, and some friends took me to see a new young singer they were raving about at a local club on West Eighth Street called the Bon Soir. Before she came on to sing, a small troupe of comics did a parody of *Psycho* that was really quite scary. Shadows of a shower curtain and a huge plunging knife were thrown against the back wall of the club while eerie music was played, and then all the lights went out and everyone started screaming. It was pandemonium for a few moments, and I wondered how the teenage girl who stepped up to the microphone could follow such an act and gain control of the room, but after just a few notes, Barbra Streisand had us in the palm of her hand. But I still recall that the *Psycho* bit was very effective; it had *me* screaming, because the movie was still so fresh in my mind."

Parodies and nightclub takeoffs of *Psycho* surfaced almost immediately upon release of the film. (Television comedy and variety shows tended to leave the picture alone, as its content was considered a bit controversial at the time for the home screen.)

But it was, of course, in motion pictures that its immediate, and lasting, impact was felt most keenly. Many films that followed *Psycho* into theaters were influenced by its plot, characters, and atmosphere, while others simply ripped off its title.

One of Hitchcock's misleading publicity stills. In the film, Marion doesn't go near Mrs. Bates's rocker.

"*Homicidal* is the first and most obvious *Psycho* imitation," writes Michael Weldon in the amusingly titled *Psychotronic Encyclopedia of Film*. Released in 1961 by director William Castle, *Homicidal* is a slow-moving yet oddly compelling tale in which actress Jean Arless plays a woman named Emily and her husband Warren, with only partial success. There is a brutal stabbing murder early in the film, and later a decapitation on a staircase.

Other pictures reminiscent of *Psycho* made during the sixties and seventies include *Anatomy of a Psycho; The Couch; Die! Die! My Darling; Hypnosis; Paranoiac; Psycho-Circus; Mania; Phobia; The Psycho Lover; Psychomania; The Psychopath; Pyro; Dementia 13;* and *Deranged,* a 1974 epic based on the Ed Gein murders. To some degree the box-office success of *Psycho* also paved the way for Robert Aldrich's Bette Davis vehicles, *What Ever Happened to Baby Jane?* and *Hush . . . Hush, Sweet Charlotte,* as well as for *Berserk!* and *Strait-Jacket,* two of Joan Crawford's final films. (On a lighter note, Mel Brooks took comic pot shots at *Psycho* in *High Anxiety,* while Brian De Palma—frequently criticized for blatantly emulating Hitchcock—created a memorable shower scene of his own in *Dressed to Kill.*)

And ironically, though Hitchcock prided himself in the clever way he *implied* terrible violence in *Psycho* without resorting to gross explicitness, the picture encouraged other filmmakers to push violent content to new, graphic extremes. If Hitch had gotten away with the shower murder, they reasoned, it would now be possible to take things even further. *Blood Feast,* for example, directed by cult favorite Herschell Gordon Lewis and released a scant three years after *Psycho,* is generally considered to be the "first gore film." Within the plot, a girl's head is ripped open on a beach, and the tongue, brains, and a leg are surgically removed in "disgusting and convincing full-color detail."

When *Psycho* opened, some critics took Hitchcock to task for having ushered in an unwelcome new era in screen violence. And thanks to filmmakers in Hitchcock's wake, who felt little need to practice his restraint, the criticisms, unfortunately, proved well-founded.

By the time Jamie Lee Curtis starred in John Carpenter's *Halloween* and its first sequel (in 1978 and 1981, respectively), "slasher" movies—usually involving imperiled teenagers—were commonplace, and audiences had become alarmingly desensitized to increasingly graphic on-screen killing. The horrors of *Psycho* seemed tame by comparison. When Jamie Lee saw her mother's most famous scene for the first time, she found it "not jarring or shocking at all."

As *Psycho*'s reputation grew over the years, it became one of the most dissected and analyzed movies in history. Serious film writers pored over every frame of the film in search not only of the technical secrets utilized in its creation, but also looking for subtle (if not actually subliminal), meanings they suspected were lurking in almost every facet of the picture. Some of the published conclusions reached after these intense studies are meritorious.

In *The Art of Alfred Hitchcock,* Donald Spoto asserts that there is significance in the choice of the painting hanging on the Bates Motel office wall that conceals the peephole Norman uses to spy on Marion Crane as she disrobes in preparation for her shower. Spoto writes, "Norman removes from the wall a replica of *Susanna and the Elders,* the biblical story of three old men who spied on a righteous woman as she prepared for her bath, and then, passions aflame, leaped out at her with threats of sexual blackmail. Norman, in other words, removes the *artifact* of deadly voyeurism and replaces it with the *act* itself."

William Rothman, in his fascinating, in-depth study, *Hitchcock: The Murderous Gaze,* discusses a recurring visual motif he notices in virtually all of the director's films. Describing it as a "pattern of parallel vertical lines: Hitchcock's | | | |," Rothman says it is represented by stairway banisters in *The Lodger* and *Shadow of a Doubt,* and by the back of a chair in *The 39 Steps.* Rothman asserts that the motif symbolizes imprisonment—particularly of a sexual nature—and is seen prominently in *Psycho*'s opening title graphics, as designed by Saul Bass. It *is* known that Bass and Hitchcock held meetings to discuss the title artwork, but how specific Hitch was in his suggestions for the design is lost to posterity.

Rothman also claims that Norman stutters slightly on the word "mattress" when he is showing Marion around her motel room, because the word is akin to matricide. However, upon viewing the film, one sees that Norman says "mattress" casually, with no hint of a stutter. Rothman further proposes that some of the electric lights seen in *Psycho* represent Mother Bates: "Again and again," Rothman writes, "a lamp will be associated with the mother, becoming her surrogate . . . and the emblem of her mystery."

In *Hitchcock and Homosexuality,* author Theodore Price puts forth a hypothesis which concludes that Hitch was repulsed and fascinated in equal measure by homosexuality and the Jack the Ripper murders, and that both subjects influenced what material he chose to film and the manner in which he presented it.

One completely erroneous rumor concerning hidden meanings in *Psycho* claims that Hitch chose the name Bates Motel because the initials B.M. played into the scatological aspect of his sense of humor. Of course, it was Robert Bloch, not Hitchcock, who originated the name Bates in his original novel, written in 1958.

Given how intellectually curious and well-read Hitchcock was, and taking into account his desire to create multilayered films that would bear repeated viewings, one must assume that some of the theories put forth about the psychological and intellectual shadings seen in his films have validity. But often, what appears to have been carefully thought out is, in fact, unintentional." Sometimes a cigar," Freud is alleged to have said, "is just a cigar."

Hilton Green, for one, is skeptical about much of the cerebral musings that cling to Hitchcock's work. "Some of this stuff gets a little far-out," he says, laughing. "If he had indulged in most of it, he never would have had time to actually make a movie."

Of the movies Hitch did make following *Psycho,* only *The*

Birds in 1963 came close to making as much money or generating as much excitement. (His tag line for the movie, *"The Birds Is Coming,"* is a classic.) *Marnie* in 1964, though not particularly well received upon release, has acquired staunch supporters, and Hitch's 1972 effort *Frenzy* was hailed by critics as the master's return to form following the tepid spy-themed mysteries *Torn Curtain* in 1966 and *Topaz* three years later. His final picture, *Family Plot*—made when he was seventy-six years old—was seen as an entertaining return to the lighter fare he had favored in *To Catch a Thief* and *The Trouble with Harry.*

One might ponder what Hitchcock would have thought of the three sequels to *Psycho,* the first of which appeared in 1983, three years after his death. In *Psycho II,* Norman Bates is released from a mental institution, with the result that fresh murders follow, and a surprise ending ensues. Along with Tony Perkins re-creating Norman, Vera Miles enacted Lila Crane for a second time, but Robert Loggia assumed the role of Sam, as John Gavin was engaged as President Reagan's ambassador to Mexico. Perkins directed *Psycho III* in 1986, which placed Norman rather on the periphery of the story line, and *Psycho IV,* again with Perkins as Norman, was produced for TV. Hilton Green, their producer, recognizes that the quality of the films vary, but he's proud of Tony Perkins's contributions and also of the fact that he made *Psycho II* for $4 million. "We put every cent of it on the screen, too," Green says. "None of it ended up on the cutting room floor"—an accomplishment the businessman in Hitchcock would have no doubt cheered.

Character actor Donovan Scott recalls working in *Psycho III* with fondness: "Tony Perkins was wonderful. He knew, of course, the character of Norman like no one else, so it was fun to watch him slip into the role with such ease. And, being an actor made him a generous director because he realized what the other actor's needs were. I think he was a very versatile talent, and I really enjoyed being a part of the film."

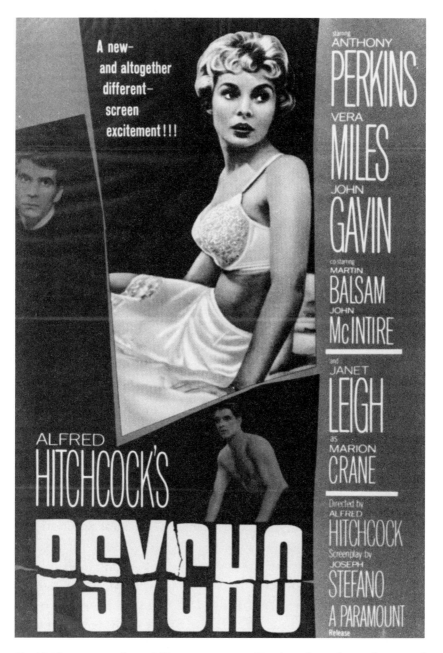

In 1960, a pastor from Minnesota wrote Hitchcock to decry the use of this sexy poster art because "'children would be exposed to it.'"

But nothing ever equaled the original *Psycho*. And if tangible proof is needed of its impact on popular culture, it can be found in any movie memorabilia shop, where one can buy numerous items emblazoned with "Bates Motel," including drinking cups and tumblers, hand towels, key chains, cocktail napkins, and swizzle sticks. In the film, Norman points to the desk in Marion's room and says cheerily, "There's stationery with 'Bates Motel' printed on it in case you want to make your friends back home feel envious." Now, those friends can purchase notepads with the motel logo. Still photos, lobby cards, and posters from *Psycho* are highly collected: A 27-by-41-inch one-sheet poster from the film is currently valued at $750. In 1992, the Innovative Corporation publishing house released a series of comic books that depict every scene in the film, and Mrs. Bates's corpse is on display at the Planet Hollywood restaurant in Las Vegas.

No other murder mystery in the history of the movies has inspired such merchandising. (To say nothing of the popular displays at the Universal theme parks in California and Florida.) Does such commercial exploitation lessen the importance of *Psycho*? No more than such merchandising cheapens the worthiness of *E.T.* or *Beauty and the Beast,* which is to say not at all. Alfred Hitchcock would, in fact, probably get a kick out of the lasting commercial appeal of the film—provided he received a percentage of the profits! If such merchandising had been as common a tool in film promotion in 1960 as it is now, Hitch would surely have taken advantage of it, brilliant promotional showman that he was.

As indirectly important as television was in the production of *Psycho,* the medium itself proved to be unwelcoming to the movie at first. In May 1964, NBC wanted to license an airing of the film, but Paramount sent a memo to Hitchcock suggesting a reissue to theaters instead. Agreeing with Paramount, Hitch successfully rereleased *Psycho* the following year, after which CBS paid Paramount $450,000 to screen the movie in prime time early in the 1966 fall season.

On September 19, three days before the scheduled airing, Valerie Percy, the 21-year-old daughter of Illinois senatorial candidate Charles Percy, was murdered in the family home in the Chicago suburb of Kenilworth. The academically gifted coed had been stabbed twelve times with a double-edged knife in her bedroom while her parents slept in their room, just feet away. Although Valerie's mother saw the killer briefly as he rushed from the scene, he was never identified, and the case remains open to this day.

CBS immediately began receiving requests from the Midwest to drop the scheduled showing of *Psycho* in deference to the tragedy. The network agreed to "postpone the airing until later in the year," but ultimately, the film was never shown over network television.

In 1970 (following still another successful reissue in theaters a year earlier), *Psycho* went to syndicated (local) television stations across the country (as part of a package of Universal films), where it was shown with frequency until 1990. At that time, it was leased to cable stations for two years, and in 1993, it once again went out in syndication as part of a group of films from Universal known as the "List of a Lifetime" package. This current lease agreement will play out in June 1997. As with any fine film, however, *Psycho* should be viewed away from commercial television if possible. The various edits—now done more for the insertion of commercials than for censorship requirements—distract greatly from the pace and carefully choreographed suspense of the movie.

As Janet has said, her one regret about having made *Psycho* is that its enormous impact prevented her from working with Hitchcock again, so identified was she with Marion Crane.

Of course, Janet was offered any number of *Psycho*-like

thrillers over the years, which she wisely turned down. Instead, she chose to continue playing a variety of parts in a number of interesting projects. First, she joined a long list of guest stars in glorified cameo roles in *Pepe,* a rambling comedy that failed to launch a Hollywood career for its star, the popular Mexican comedian, Cantinflas.

In 1962, *The Manchurian Candidate* placed Janet within a cast that included Frank Sinatra, Laurence Harvey, and Angela Lansbury in a chilling, cautionary cold-war tale of political assassination. As one of the film's producers. Sinatra pulled it from distribution a year later after the murder of President Kennedy. It remained unseen for many years, but when it reemerged in the early eighties, it was immediately hailed as a classic that was as brilliant and disturbing as it had been twenty years earlier.

The following year, Janet enjoyed a change of pace—her first musical comedy since 1955. In a bouffant black wig, she was Rosie, the vivacious and patient girlfriend of Dick Van Dyke in the movie version of the Broadway smash *Bye Bye Birdie.* In one frantic number, she got tossed around by a roomful of overzealous Shriner types (a photo from the scene put her on the cover of *Life* magazine for the second time). She sang along with Van Dyke in "Put On a Happy Face," and joined costars Ann-Margret and Bobby Rydell for a wistful version of "One Boy." Later that year, she reunited with her first-ever leading man, Van Johnson, in the sophisticated romantic comedy *Wives and Lovers.*

Following her wedding to Robert Brandt, Janet cut back on film work, preferring instead to throw her considerable energies behind her new marriage, her work on behalf of the United States Informational Services and the National Advisory Council for the Peace Corps, her numerous charitable endeavors, and the upbringing of her two young daughters.

Of the handful of films Janet made during the sixties and seventies, one standout is 1966's *Harper,* with Paul Newman as an updated forties-style gumshoe. *An American Dream* in the same year was a stylish drama based on the novel by Norman Mailer, and her costar was the erstwhile Sam Loomis hopeful, Stuart Whitman. In 1972 she supported Trish Van Devere in *One Is a Lonely Number,* a well-received study of the aftereffects of divorce, and in 1979 she appeared with Ruth Gordon and Lee Strasberg in *Boardwalk* and with her daughter Jamie Lee in John Carpenter's thriller *The Fog.*

During this time, Janet also found unusual acting challenges on television. She has made a number of TV movies—*House on Green Apple Road,* which first aired in 1968, is considered one of the best ever—and she has appeared effectively as a guest star on shows ranging from *The Smothers Brothers Comedy Hour,* on which she hilariously played a young woman at a glamorous full-dress ball who is only slightly hampered by having to drag a third leg around the dance floor, to *Columbo,* in which she portrayed a faded movie star who murders her wealthy husband to finance an ill-conceived comeback.

Janet's decision to pull back on her acting career proved to be a smart one. While some of her contemporaries are frustrated in their struggle to find decent roles, and others are forced to accept work doing commercial endorsements, Janet enjoys a full and fruitful life that isn't centered on a hoped-for call from a casting agent. She returns to acting when a project intrigues her, and she is enormously involved with charitable work.

Janet takes tremendous pride in the accomplishments of her two actress daughters, and she is a doting grandmother. Bob Brandt confirms that *Psycho* is the film his business associates most frequently ask about when they learn the identity of his wife. "Janet is always so pleasant with people when they come up to her. She's never rude, always has time to chat and sign autographs, and I think people appreciate that."

For this book, Jamie Lee Curtis finally admitted that she had never seen *Psycho* from start to finish and had been fibbing for years about watching it against her mother's wishes when she

A informal family gathering with Janet, Bob, Kelly, and Jamie Lee.

was a little girl. "When I first became an actress, at eighteen, I was always asked a lot of questions about my parents," she says. "And they would always ask about *Psycho* and when my mom died in the shower, and I hadn't really seen the film, but I was asked about it so often that I finally made up a story about being eleven or something and that it was on *The Late Show* and that I set my alarm and stayed up, or woke up late and secretly watched *Psycho*. And as the story went, I ran into her room screaming, 'Mommy! Mommy!' You know, after the shower scene. Well, the truth of the matter is I still don't think I've ever seen the movie all the way through. You know, *I hate* horror movies. I don't watch them. That's probably why I've never seen *Psycho*, because I don't like to be frightened. I never have. I'm a very sensitive creature."

Kelly Curtis has also never seen a full version of *Psycho*, but for a slightly different reason. When she was very small, she recalls, "The family was sitting around watching my mom's movie *Two Tickets to Broadway*. There's a scene where her character decides to give up her hope for Broadway stardom [and the love of Tony Martin] and return to her hometown. In her boardinghouse, she's packing to leave and she's so unhappy. I remember she throws her favorite dress on the floor or something, and she seemed so sad that I started to cry."

Janet realized that her daughter was too young to distinguish between her on-screen persona and the mom she knew at home, and if Kelly reacted this sensitively to a brief scene in an innocuous musical, Janet decided, *Psycho* would be out of the question for a few years. Kelly has still not seen *Psycho,* and is under the impression that it is gorier than it actually is. "It will probably be anticlimactic when I do see the film," she laughs.

In 1984, Janet published her autobiography, *There Really Was a Hollywood,* and found that the challenge of focusing her creativity on the printed page was one she greatly enjoyed. Now, writing has become an exciting new career for her. Her first novel, *House of Destiny,* is set for publication in the United States in the fall of 1995. A multigenerational saga that climaxes in Hollywood, the book has already been set for publication in five foreign countries.

As I had anticipated, it was a great pleasure working with Janet Leigh on this project. Not only was it enlightening to discover along with her the singular hold *Psycho* continues to have on the public consciousness, but the affection and respect she inspires in Hollywood made my job so much easier than it most certainly would have been without her. Sometimes just the mention of her name opened doors and allowed access that would have been extremely difficult, if not impossible, to obtain otherwise.

Jamie Lee Curtis wrote a charming preface to her mother's

autobiography in which she mentioned how often people on a film set tell her that they had also worked with Janet and how much they admired her. "Your mother is one of the few people in Hollywood," they tell her, "that no one has anything bad to say about." After working on this project for eighteen months, I can certainly understand why.

C.N.

A CLOSING NOTE

I am deeply grateful to my co-author, Christopher Nickens, for making the writing of this book such a rewarding experience. Together we have followed the fascinating trail of *Psycho* bread crumbs that led us to the secrets of the house behind the Bates Motel.

As for me, I am forever indebted to an industry that has given me such a full and good life. I know I've worked hard, but a lot of people have worked hard and have not been rewarded as I have. I have touched titans and titans have touched me. There is no substitute for that kind of fulfillment.

Alfred Hitchcock may not have won the Oscar for any of his five nominations, but in 1967, the Academy of Motion Picture Arts and Sciences presented him with the Irving G. Thalberg Memorial Award, given for consistently high quality of production. Amen!

In the spring of 1974, the Film Society of Lincoln Center honored Alfred Hitchcock. I was so proud to be able to pay homage to this wonderful man. And to be included in the company of such artists as Princess Grace of Monaco, François Truffaut, Joan Fontaine, Teresa Wright and so many others was icing on the cake.

Then came 1979, when the Life Achievement Award of the American Film Institute went to Alfred Hitchcock. And when Anthony Perkins and I were able to show our esteem for our beloved friend together.

Thank God for giving knowledge to Man, who could then create film so generations to come could enjoy and reap the benefits provided by the greats of the past.

ACKNOWLEDGMENTS

Jim Arnold	Paramount
Robert Bloch	Author of *Psycho*
David Block	Beverly Hills Videocentre
Bob Brandt	Husband of Janet Leigh
Rene Clinkunbroomer	MCA/Universal
Chris Coslick	*Hollywood Reporter*
Jamie Lee Curtis	Daughter of Janet Leigh
Kelly Curtis	Daughter of Janet Leigh
Corinne De Luca	MCA/Universal
Mary Ann Fortuna	MCA/Universal
John Gavin	Actor, ambassador, businessman
Tom Gilbert	*Variety*
Sam Gill	Special Collections Department at the Academy of Motion Picture Arts and Sciences
Graziella	Secretary to Mr. and Mrs. Perkins
Hilton Green	Price Entertainment
Gunver Haas	National Screen Service
Curtis Harrington	Film Director
Wendy Keyes	Lincoln Center Film Society
A. C. Lyles	Paramount
Eric D. Madden	Collector
Mrs. Berry Perkins	Widow of Anthony Perkins
Elvis Perkins	Son of Anthony Perkins
Osgood Perkins	Son of Anthony Perkins
Robbie Pierson	Secretary to Janet Leigh
Marilyn Reiss	Public Relations
Greg Rice	Paramount
Rita Riggs	Costumer of *Psycho*
Lyn Rowland	MCA/Universal

Donovan Scott	Actor/director
Lillian Burns Sidney	Adviser to Janet Leigh
John Springer	Author, Public Relations
The Staffs	Film Studies Libraries at UCLA, USC, and the American Film Institute
Joseph Stefano	Scriptwriter of *Psycho;* producer
Herb Steinberg	MCA/Universal
Ada Tesar	Secretary to Janet Leigh
Robert J. Wagner	Actor/Producer
Lew Wasserman	MCA/Universal
Wendy Williamson	Public Relations, Northwest Chamber Orchestra

And for their friendship, encouragement, understanding, and talent, we are grateful to: Loretta Barrett, Les Burke, Mark Calvin, Marc Drotman, Anne Francis, Nicholas Gunn, Mike Hawks, Bill Klausing, Randy Lunsford, Gerson Michaelson, Tim Newth, John Sala, Coyne Steven Sanders, Robert Scott, Allison and Leslie Solow, James Spada, Karen Swenson, Laura Van Wormer, Guy Vespoint, George Zeno, and Shaye Areheart and everyone at Harmony Books.

Selected Bibliography

Anobile, Richard J. *Alfred Hitchcock's Psycho*. New York: Universe Books, 1974.

Bloch, Robert. *Psycho*. New York: Warner Books, 1959.

Bloch, Robert. *Once Around the Bloch*. New York: Tor, 1993.

Bouzereau, Laurent. *The Alfred Hitchcock Quote Book*. New York: Citadel, 1993.

Eames, John Douglas. *The MGM Story*. New York: Crown, 1975.

Freeman, David. *The Last Days of Alfred Hitchcock*. New York: The Overlook Press, 1984.

Harmetz, Aljean. *Round Up the Usual Suspects*. New York: Hyperion, 1992.

Hurley, Neil P. *Soul in Suspense: Hitchcock's Fright and Delight*. New Jersey: The Scarecrow Press, 1993.

Kapsis, Robert E. *Hitchcock: The Making of a Reputation*. Chicago: The University of Chicago Press, 1992.

Kunhardt, Phillip B., Jr., editor. *Life: The First Fifty Years*. New York: Time, Inc., 1986.

Leigh, Janet. *There Really Was a Hollywood*. New York: Doubleday, 1984.

McCarty, John and Brian Kelleher. *Alfred Hitchcock Presents*. New York: St Martin's Press, 1985.

Price, Theodore. *Hitchcock and Homosexuality*. New Jersey: The Scarecrow Press, 1992.

Rebello, Stephen. *Alfred Hitchcock and the Making of Psycho*. New York: Dembner, 1990.

Rothman, William. *Hitchcock and the Murderous Gaze*. Massachusetts: Harvard University Press, 1982.

Schechter, Harold. *Deviant: The Shocking True Story of the Original Psycho*. New York: Pocket Books, 1991.

Spada, James. *Grace: The Secret Lives of a Princess*. New York: Doubleday, 1987.

Spoto, Donald. *The Art of Alfred Hitchcock*. New York: Doubleday, 1979.

Truffaut, Francois. *Hitchcock/Truffaut*. New York: Simon & Schuster, 1967.

Weldon, Michael. *The Psychotronic Encyclopedia of Film*. New York: Ballantine Books, 1983.

PHOTO CREDITS

Christopher Nickens is the author of biographies of Elizabeth Taylor, Bette Davis, Marlon Brando, and Natalie Wood. He lives in Los Angeles, where he is preparing a biography of Joan Crawford.

791.4372 Leigh, Janet.
L
    Psycho.

22.00

WITHDRAWN

DATE			